OKANAGAN COLLEGE

P9-DTN-077

EFFECTIVE COLLEGE TEACHING: FRESH INSIGHTS AND EXEMPLARY PRACTICES

LIBRARY
BRITISH COLUM

OKANAGAN COLLEGE
LIBRARY
BRITISH COLUMBIA

EFFECTIVE COLLEGE TEACHING: FRESH INSIGHTS AND EXEMPLARY PRACTICES

EDWIN RALPH (EDITOR)

Nova Science Publishers, Inc.
New York

Senior Editors: Susan Boriotti and Donna Dennis
Coordinating Editor: Tatiana Shohov
Office Manager: Annette Hellinger
Graphics: Wanda Serrano
Editorial Production: Vladimir Klestov, Matthew Kozlowski and Maya Columbus
Circulation: Ave Maria Gonzalez, Vera Popovic, Luis Aviles, Raymond Davis,
            Melissa Diaz and Jeannie Pappas
Communications and Acquisitions: Serge P. Shohov
Marketing: Cathy DeGregory

Library of Congress Cataloging-in-Publication Data
Available Upon Request

ISBN 1-59033-655-0

Copyright © 2003 by Nova Science Publishers, Inc.
         400 Oser Ave, Suite 1600
         Hauppauge, New York 11788-3619
         Tele.: 631-231-7269   Fax: 631-231-8175
         e-mail: Novascience@earthlink.net
         Web Site: http://www.novapublishers.com

All rights reserved. No part of this book may be reproduced, stored in a retrieval system or transmitted in any form or by any means: electronic, electrostatic, magnetic, tape, mechanical photocopying, recording or otherwise without permission from the publishers.

The authors and publisher have taken care in preparation of this book, but make no expressed or implied warranty of any kind and assume no responsibility for any errors or omissions. No liability is assumed for incidental or consequential damages in connection with or arising out of information contained in this book.

This publication is designed to provide accurate and authoritative information with regard to the subject matter covered herein. It is sold with the clear understanding that the publisher is not engaged in rendering legal or any other professional services. If legal or any other expert assistance is required, the services of a competent person should be sought. FROM A DECLARATION OF PARTICIPANTS JOINTLY ADOPTED BY A COMMITTEE OF THE AMERICAN BAR ASSOCIATION AND A COMMITTEE OF PUBLISHERS.

Printed in the United States of America

CONTENTS

INTRODUCTION

Edwin G. Ralph

College of Education
University of Saskatchewan
Saskatoon, Saskatchewan, Canada

During the past decade there has been a notable growth of interest in the enhancement of instruction in post-secondary institutions in many countries. (Tuijnman, 1996; Veld, Fussel, and Neave, 1996). Although teaching has always been one of the three fundamental components of the work of the professoriat in universities and colleges (together with research and service), its relative importance has dramatically increased in recent years (Boyer, 1990).

Evidence of this growth has been shown on three fronts: (a) by a proliferation of new books, journals, and articles published on various aspects of the teaching/learning process in higher education; (b) by an expansion in the number of national and international professional associations and conferences related to the teaching enterprise; and (c) by the establishment in many post-secondary institutions of special offices or centers devoted to the enhancement of the teaching function, particularly at the undergraduate level.

A major thrust of this current interest and activity in instructional development has been to promote teaching effectiveness, and thus to improve student learning (e.g., American Association, 1997; Barr & Tagg, 1995; Lazerson & Wagener, 1999). In other words, post-secondary institutions are seeking to help all instructional personnel - whether they are professors, graduate teaching assistants, part-time lecturers, sessional instructors, laboratory demonstrators, tutorial directors, seminar leaders, discussion coordinators, or other personnel working in *any* facet of the teaching/learning enterprise - to better their classroom practice.

Yet, the three often-asked and debated questions related to this whole subject still arise: What is effective teaching? How can it be measured and/or assessed? and Can individuals acquire and/or enhance these skills, and if so, how?

The purpose of this volume is not to address the philosophical and theoretical bases underlying these basic questions; nor is it to summarize the voluminous body of educational literature that is being accumulated and that is furnishing growing empirical evidence and sound research results addressing these three key questions. Although seeking to explore such purposes is worthy and necessary, the major goal of this book is to provide readers with fresh and practical insights about excellent teaching at the college level, and to present particular examples of it.

The authors of the chapters in this volume have themselves been nominees and/or recipients of educational awards in their particular fields of undergraduate teaching. I asked them to share, in practical terms, some of their actual teaching practices and/or related research findings. They thus created these chapters with the objectives of helping inform readers' own instructional behaviors, by providing insight and understanding in either adopting some of these "new" instructional approaches or in adapting them to match readers' individual contexts.

In Chapter 1, Gusthart and Harrison summarize their recent research results describing what several groups of undergraduate students from four different colleges at one Western Canadian university desired to see in their instructors' teaching. Their findings are not unlike those from previous research examining students' perspectives.

In Chapter 2, Kalyn and Krohn describe their highly successful *Project Move* dance program, in which they prepare novice instructors to teach contemporary dance to middle-years students in public schools. Their research on *Project Move* reveals that *all* participants experience growth both in competence and confidence -- in their respective areas of endeavour.

Karl Baumgardner, in Chapter 3, describes how to implement the "Inquiry Approach" in teaching a social sciences course. He illustrates how *any* instructor could adapt the key principles of inquiry to fit the context of *any* subject at *any* level in order to stimulate motivation and enhance cognition in his/her classroom interaction.

In Chapter 4, Dimmock describes how he has successfully implemented a "Problem Solving Approach" in the teaching of two of his Pharmacy courses. His students have repeatedly reported that they find this method of learning to be stimulating, challenging, and rewarding.

Smith, in Chapter 5, encourages instructors to incorporate the "*Synectics Approach*" (i.e., the use of extended metaphoric comparisons) in their courses for the purposes of encouraging creative and critical thinking on the part of both instructor and students, and of breaking out of familiar but sometimes stagnant cognitive patterns.

In Chapter 6, Mills invites college instructors to apply "Cooperative Learning" to their teaching. Mills advocates that teachers adopt the principles, as outlined - or that they modify part or all of them to match their particular instructional situations. She has found that the implementation of cooperative learning has consistently proven fruitful both in her own teaching and in the numerous instructional workshops that she has presented.

Roy-Neysmith and McNinch, in Chapter 7, summarize their recent research findings regarding the use of students' mid-term course evaluations to improve the effectiveness of the small-group seminar component of one course, and the seminar-leaders' performance in it. Their results suggest fresh insights for administrators and course leaders to consider as they seek to improve tutorials.

In Chapter 8, Zulkoskey describes a unique instructional approach he has successfully implemented in a first-year Physics course. His students reported that they found his *"Peer Teaching/Group Learning"* method to be a refreshing and stimulating change from the traditional lecture format, to which they had been accustomed.

Finally, in Chapter 9, I draw some key implications from the eight chapters to assist instructional personnel at *any* level in *all* fields to improve their professional competence.

*   *   *   *   *

All of the authors in this volume are respected teachers and are distinguished in their respective fields, as demonstrated by their nomination for and/or receipt of various teaching awards throughout their careers. The overarching aim of their contributions to this book is to provide -- for *anyone* interested in the area of instructional development in post-secondary education (particularly for those who may be beginning their teaching careers) -- a set of proven, practical guidelines. The authors' desire is that these teaching experiences may provide readers with suggestions to scrutinize, points to ponder, techniques to try, critiques to consider, and approaches to apply as they seek to improve their own professional practice.

REFERENCES

American Association for High Education. (1997). *Assessing impact: Evidence and action* (Presentations from the 1997 AAHE Conference on Assessment & Quality). Washington, DC: Author.

Barr, R., & Tagg, J. (1995). From teaching to learning: A new paradigm for undergraduate education. *Change, 27*(6), 13-25.

Boyer, E. (1990). *Scholarship reconsidered: Priorities of the professoriate.* Menlo Park, CA: Carnegie Foundation for the Advancement of Teaching.

Lazerson, M., & Wagener, U. (1999). Teaching and learning the unfamiliar. *Change, 31*(1), 38-39.

Tuijnman, A. (Ed.). (1996). *International encyclopedia of adult education and training* (2nd ed.). New York: Elsevier Science.

Veld, R., Fussel, H., & Neave, G. (Eds.). (1996). *Relations between state and higher education.* Boston: Kluwer Law International.

Chapter 1

THE GLOBAL ASSESSMENT
OF TEACHING EFFECTIVENESS

Len Gusthart
College of Education
University of Saskatchewan
Saskatoon, Saskatchewan, Canada
Paul Harrison
Darla Moore School of Business
University of South Carolina

ABSTRACT

In this study the authors surveyed students from four different colleges at one Western Canadian university in order to determine the factors students believe to be important in instructors' teaching effectiveness. Analysis of the data showed that students highly valued four dimensions: the extent of students' learning, the teachers' enthusiasm, the teachers' organization and preparation, and the fair evaluation of students' work.

INTRODUCTION

The status of teaching in higher education is currently in a period of change in which teaching is being seen as increasingly more important relative to the research mission of higher education (Boyer & Rice, 1990).

The renewed emphasis being placed on teaching in the university necessitates that effective and credible measures of teaching effectiveness be developed and used. Traditionally, student ratings of teaching have been the predominant mechanism employed to evaluate teaching in the university setting (Feldman, 1989).

One of the debates over the use of student evaluations of teaching effectiveness deals with whether an overall rating or factorial dimensions of teaching effectiveness should be used in personnel decisions. Some researchers support the use of overall ratings of teacher effectiveness (Abrami, 1989) through the utilization of a set of global rating items on the evaluation instrument itself or, if necessary, through an unweighted average of the individual factors in a rating instrument. However, other researchers argue that teaching is multidimensional (Marsh & Hocevar, 1991), and that the individual dimensions should be considered separately in evaluating teaching effectiveness. These researchers assert that if an overall rating of teaching effectiveness is to be used at all, the overall rating should be a weighted average of the individual factors, with the weights being determined by logical and empirical analysis.

Ryan and Harrison (1995) conducted a policy capturing study where students made overall evaluations of hypothetical instructors based on a manipulation of the teaching factors from Marsh's work. The results indicated that the factorial dimensions were salient and that they differentially influence the overall evaluation that students assign to instructors. The major objective of the present study is to extend Ryan and Harrison's (1995) work to a different set of students at a Canadian university.

BACKGROUND

Overall vs. Multidimensional Evaluations

A major issue frequently debated in teacher evaluation research and practice deals with the relative merits of using an overall evaluation versus a multi-dimensional profile of teaching effectiveness (Marsh, 1991). For personnel decisions, there is considerable debate as to whether a single score is more useful and appropriate than a profile of scores reflecting multiple dimensions (Marsh, 1991).

Abrami and d'Apollonia (1991) favor the use of several global items to evaluate teaching for personnel decisions. On the other side of the issue, Frey (1978) argues that only individual teaching dimensions should be considered and he favors excluding global rating items from evaluation instruments.

Marsh and his colleagues (Marsh & Hocevar, 1991; Marsh and Dunkin, 1992) have chosen a middle ground between these two positions, recommending the use of both specific dimensions and global ratings. Marsh feels that it is important to differentially weight the specific dimensions. These weights could be constructed on the basis of empirical research findings or ratings of the relative importance of specific components by the department head, a promotions committee, or the instructor.

Weighted-Average Approach to Computing Overall Evaluations

Marsh and Roche (1993) evaluated the effectiveness of students' evaluations of teaching effectiveness (SETEs) as a means for enhancing university teaching. Their research used a weighted average approach in arriving at an overall evaluation of teaching effectiveness. The individual dimensions in Marsh's instrument were weighted in relative importance by the teacher being evaluated. Thus, Marsh and Roche (1993) were able to construct a teacher-rated importance weighted average of the dimensions in arriving at an overall evaluation.

RESEARCH METHODS

It is apparent that overall evaluations of teaching effectiveness are used in personnel decisions in many universities. While there have been studies which have computed an overall evaluation through the use of a weighted average (Marsh and Roche, 1993), Ryan and Harrison's (1995) work was the first study to examine systematically how students weight various teaching factors in arriving at their overall evaluation of teaching effectiveness. This present study's objective was to determine the relative importance that students in different instructional contexts at one university place on individual teaching factors in assigning a single value as an overall evaluation of teaching effectiveness.

Policy Capturing Approach

A policy capturing approach was used to determine the relative importance of various teaching factors to students' overall evaluations of teaching effectiveness. In this approach, a dependent variable or decision variable is defined. In this research, the dependent/decision variable is the students' overall ratings on a scale from 1 to 9 for a set of hypothetical instructor profiles.

A set of independent variables or cue variables is also defined. In this research, the independent/cue variables are the nine teaching factors in the Student Evaluation of Educational Quality (SEEQ) developed by Marsh and Hocevar (1991). These factors are: 1) Learning, 2) Enthusiasm, 3) Organization, 4) Group Interaction, 5) Individual Rapport, 6) Breadth of Coverage, 7) Examination Fairness, 8) Assignments, and 9) Course Difficulty. Values of 0=Low and 1=High were assigned to the SEEQs/cue variables and presented to the students in a questionnaire. Subjects then assigned an overall evaluation to the dependent/ decision variable based on the combination of values they were given for the independent/cue variables. Subjects repeated this process over several combinations of values for the cue variables.

The values students assigned to the decision variable were regressed onto the values of the cue variables and the resulting regression coefficients indicated the relative influence each cue variable had on the value students assigned to the decision variable. In this research, students assigned an overall rating (1-9) for different hypothetical instructor profiles defined by the various combinations of "Low" (0) and "High" (1) assigned to the nine SEEQs.

Task and Experimental Design

Each subject received a set of materials that included: 1) a description of each of the factors of teaching effectiveness identified in Marsh's SEEQ, 2) a set of instructions, and 3) a set of 32 hypothetical instructor profiles. The profiles contained the nine factors of teaching effectiveness identified in the SEEQ discussed earlier. Thirty two hypothetical instructor profiles were used with each of the teaching factors varied at two levels, high or low. Each teaching factor appeared 16 times as "low", and 16 times as "high".

The participants were told to read carefully the description of each of the nine teaching factors in Marsh's SEEQ. The education students were then given the following written instructions:

You are to place yourself in the position of a student enrolled in an education course at this university. Each of the cases given below describe a hypothetical education instructor at this university. After you read through the information given in each case pertaining to the hypothetical instructor's performance, you are to give a global evaluation pertaining to the overall level of performance of this hypothetical instructor.

Read through each case very carefully, for each case is different from every other case. Once you have finished a particular case, go on to the next one. Do *NOT* turn back to a previous case once you have started working on the next one.

If you have any questions, contact the experimenter. Thank you in advance for your cooperation.

The other three groups of subjects were given the identical instructions, except the word "education" was replaced with "sociology", "physical education", and "commerce", respectively.

The ratings were assigned on a nine point scale from 1 (very poor) to 9 (very good). Appendix A contains the descriptions of the nine teaching factors (based on the SEEQ) given to the subjects, and Appendix B contains one of the thirty-two hypothetical teacher profiles used in the study. A random order was used in presenting the descriptions of the teachings factors, and two random orders were used in presenting the thirty-two instructor profiles.

Subjects

The study was replicated in four different instructional settings in a Canadian university. Sample one consisted of Commerce (business) students ($\underline{n}$ = 53). Sample two consisted of 59 Sociology students, taking an introduction to Sociology class. Sample three consisted of 76 Education students taking a required course in educational psychology. Sample four was comprised of 30 Physical Education students taking an elective course in instructional strategies for motor skill acquisition. The decision-making exercise was filled out in class. Students were instructed to work at their own pace, and most students finished the exercise in 20 to 30 minutes. The 32 hypothetical instructor profiles were presented in two random orders; no order effects were present.

Analysis Procedures

The data analysis proceeded in two phases. In the first phase, the purpose of the analysis was: 1) to determine if the variation in the SEEQs' accounted for most of the variation in the subjects' responses, and 2) to determine the relative importance of each SEEQ in making an overall evaluation of teaching effectiveness.

Phase two of the data analyses compared results across the four instructional contexts (groups). This research focused on the data analyses that compared students from the four instructional settings. (Details of the analysis procedures are available from Dr. Len Gusthart, one of the authors of the present study. His address is indicated at the end of this chapter.)

RESULTS

The SEEQs accounted for much of the variation in the global ratings. There was a striking similarity among the orderings of the SEEQ weights across the three groups. For the Commerce, Education, and Physical Education groups, the Amount Learned had the highest weight, and it was noticeably larger than Exam Fairness, which was second. In the Sociology group, the Amount Learned and Exam Fairness were the most important and had virtually the same weights. Course Difficulty had by far the lowest relationship to the overall ratings in all four courses. Contrasts showed that the Physical Education mean was significantly different from both the Education and Sociology means.

In each course, the highest mean overall rating was given when Amount Learned was coded "High" and the lowest mean overall rating occurred when Amount Learned was coded "Low". At the other end of the scale, the mean overall rating seemed relatively unaffected by whether Course Difficulty was coded "Low" or "High". There was a significant overall group effect for Organization. The description of Organization given to students in the study was:

Organization: The instructor's explanations were clear. The course materials were well prepared and carefully explained. The proposed objectives were those actually taught so the students knew where the course was going.

These data suggest that the value of Organization in terms of contributing to the appreciation or understanding of the subject influenced the overall ratings of the Physical Education students more than it did for the other groups in this study.

DISCUSSION

This study was designed to address the process of students' evaluation of instructors and specifically what students feel are important factors or dimensions in teaching. If we can identify factors or dimensions that are prized by students, the stage may be set for helping to develop these characteristics in beginning professors. This research shows that factorial dimensions are salient and that they differentially influence the overall evaluations that students' assign to instructors and courses.

A relevant finding in this research is the consistent importance that "Amount Learned" played in shaping students' overall ratings. Amount Learned received the highest weight in three of the instructional contexts (but it was essentially the same as Exam Fairness in the Sociology context); scenarios in which Amount Learned was coded "High" received the highest overall ratings and the lowest overall ratings were assigned when Amount Learned was coded "Low". (Again, these ratings were virtually the same for both Amount Learned and Exam Fairness for the Sociology group.)

These results are similar to those found by Ryan and Harrison (1995): that Amount Learned appeared to be the most important factor influencing the overall evaluation.

Another relevant finding is the consistently small weight all four subject groups placed on Course Difficulty. This result is consistent with observations made by other researchers, suggesting that the factor of course difficulty should not enter into an overall evaluation of a teacher's performance (Abrami, 1989; Marsh, 1991).

It is important to note that a certain care is required in interpreting the differences in the weights across the four groups. Three elements are needed to describe the results fully. First, Organization was relatively more important to the Physical Education group. Second, however, was the finding that the profiles were similar across the three groups. Third, the differences in the magnitudes of the weights and similarities in the profiles of the weights appear to be more or less critical depending on how the evaluation information is to be used.

Similar profiles that differ by a magnitude of scale could possibly be used to diagnose relative strengths and weaknesses of a person's teaching. However, using such profiles to calculate a composite picture of the teaching could be problematic because two apparently similar profiles could yield significantly different composite totals.

Feldman (1989) explored the differential importance of various instructional dimensions to student achievement. His analysis indicated that the most important factors in facilitating student achievement were: clarity of teachers' explanations, preparation and organization of the course, stimulation of students' interests, motivation of students towards reaching high standards, class discussion and openness to the opinions of others, and professors' availability and helpfulness. Feldman further indicated that: Those specific instructional dimensions that are

> the most highly associated with student achievement tend to be the same ones that best discriminate among teachers with respect to the overall evaluations they receive from students (Feldman, 1989, p. 619).

The results of the present study indicate that students' perceptions of their learning is the most important factor affecting the overall evaluation students give instructors in an experimental setting. This is in contrast with the results of Cashin and Downey (1992), who found that each of two global items, one concerning the instructor, the other concerning the course, accounted for more than 50% of the variance in the weighted composite criterion measure. These findings suggest the need for further research to determine the direction of the causal relationships between individual instructional dimensions, student learning, and overall evaluations of the instructor.

An important point is to recognize the experimental nature of this present study. Students responded to hypothetical instructors in imagined classrooms. Although, the instructors were not real, this research approach was useful in studying the relationships among important constructs and the sometimes unresolvable confounding variables that influence classroom research situations. This study can also help in setting the directions for further theoretical research and for providing a focus for applied classroom research on faculty evaluation, but the results of this study cannot be generalized directly to all classroom practice.

The importance of further study in actual classroom settings is evident by examining the work of Marsh (1989), who found that overall instructor ratings were more highly correlated with instructors' enthusiasm and their lesson organization than with the aspect of student learning. This finding is different from the results reported in the current study, and requires further investigation.

Implications

The results of the present study raise several questions about what students most value in instructors' teaching. Our results are encouraging in that the students in all four instructional contexts appeared to concentrate on educationally appropriate teaching factors (i.e., Amount Learned), while largely ignoring more irrelevant factors (e.g., Course Difficulty) in assessing instructor characteristics. The students in the study were able to identify consistently what they view as important criteria in their evaluation of hypothetical instructors. The factor of "learning" rated across the four different groups as most important, with the factors of "enthusiasm" and "organization" as also being critical. In addition, the ability of instructors to evaluate the students adequately and fairly was rated as a major component, although not at the level of the first three.

These results have implications for both beginning and experienced university instructors. Students expect to learn in their classes and they prefer instructors who are enthusiastic and well organized. They also wish to be evaluated fairly and consistently by these instructors. It is possible for instructors to learn and/or to refine these skills; and consequently, faculty development should be encouraged in each of these areas.

REFERENCES

Abrami, P. C. (1989). How should we use student ratings to evaluate teaching? *Research in Higher Education, 30*(2): 221-227.

Abrami, P. C., and d'Apollonia, S. (1991). Multidimensional students' evaluations of teaching effectiveness - generalizability of "N = 1" research: Comment on Marsh (1991). *Journal of Educational Psychology, 83*: 411-415.

Boyer, E. & Rice, E. (1990). *The new American scholar* (Princeton, New Jersey: Carnegie Foundation for the Advancement of Teaching, 1990).

Cashin, W. E., and Downey, R. G. (1992). Using global student rating items for summative evaluation. *Journal of Educational Psychology, 84*: 563-572.

Feldman, K. A. (1989). Instructional effectiveness of college teachers as judged by teachers themselves, current and former students, colleagues, administrators, and external (neutral) observers. *Research in Higher Education, 30*(2): 137-194.

Frey, P. W. (1978). A two-dimensional analysis of student ratings of instruction. *Research in Higher Education, 9*: 69-91.

Marsh, H. W. (1989). Responses to reviews of students' evaluations of university teaching: Research findings, methodological issues, and directions for future research. *Instructional Evaluation, 10*: 5-9.

Marsh, H. W. (1991). Multidimensional Students' Evaluations of Teaching Effectiveness: A Test of Higher-Order Structures. *Journal of Educational Psychology, 83*: 285-296.

Marsh, H. W., & Dunkin, M. J. (1992). Students' evaluations of university teaching: A multidimensional perspective. in John. C. Smart (ed.), *Higher Education: Handbook of Theory and Research*, Volume 8, pp. 143-233. New York: Agathon Press.

Marsh, H. W., & Hocevar, D. (1991). The multidimensionality of students' evaluations of teaching effectiveness: The generality of factor structures across academic discipline, instructor level, and course level. *Teaching & Teacher Education, 7*(1): 9-18.

Marsh. H. W., and Roche, L. (1993). The use of Students' evaluations and an individually structured intervention to enhance university teaching effectiveness. *American Educational Research Journal, 30*: 217-251.

Ryan, J.M. and Harrison, P. (1995). The relationship between individual instructional characteristics and the overall assessment of teaching effectiveness across different instructional contexts. *Research in Higher Education, 36*(5): 577-594.

APPENDIX A: DESCRIPTION OF EACH FACTOR IN THE SEEQ

1. Enthusiasm: The instructor was enthusiastic about teaching the course. The instructor's style of presentation held the students interest during class.

2. Individual Rapport: The instructor was friendly towards individual students. The instructor made students feel welcome in seeking help/advice in or outside of class. The instructor was adequately accessible to students during office hours or after class.

3. Learning: Students found the course intellectually challenging and stimulating. Students learned something which they considered valuable. Students have learned and understood the subject materials in this course.

4. Course Difficulty: This compares the difficulty of this course and its workload relative to other courses.

5. Organization: The instructor's explanations were clear. The course materials were well prepared and carefully explained. The proposed objectives were those actually taught so the students knew where the course was going.

6. Breadth: The instructor contrasted the implications of various theories. The instructor presented points of view other than his/her own when appropriate. The instructor adequately discussed current developments in the field.

7. Group Interaction: The students were encouraged to participate in class. Students were invited to share their ideas and knowledge. Students were encouraged to ask questions and were given meaningful answers.

8. Assignments: The required readings/text were valuable. The readings, homework, etc. contributed to appreciation and understanding of subject.

9. Examinations: The feedback on the examinations/graded materials was valuable. The examinations/graded materials tested course content as emphasized by the instructor.

APPENDIX B: HYPOTHETICAL INSTRUCTOR SCENARIO

You are given the following information:

1. The instructor's enthusiasm in this course was   High
2. The instructor's rapport with individual students in this class was   Low
3. The amount learned in this course was   Low
4. The difficulty of this course with this instructor was   High
5. The instructor's organization in this course was   Low
6. The breadth of the material covered by the instructor in this class was   High
7. The instructor's group interaction with the students in this course was   Low
8. The value of the assignments and the textbook used in this course by the instructor were   High
9. The fairness of the examinations given by this instructor was   Low

Overall, how would you rate the classroom performance of this hypothetical instructor? **(Please circle one of the numbers below.)**

1	2	3	4	5	6	7	8	9
Very poor				Average				Very good

For information regarding details of the statistical procedures and analysis of this study, contact:

Len Gusthart
College of Kinesiology
University of Saskatchewan
105 Gymnasium Place
Saskatoon, SK Canada S7N 5C2
FAX: (306) 966-6502
E-mail: Gusthart@sask.usask.ca

Chapter 2

PROJECT MOVE!
A PRACTICAL PHYSICAL EDUCATION
LEARNING OPPORTUNITY FOR
PRE-SERVICE TEACHERS

Brenda Kalyn
College of Education
University of Saskatchewan
Saskatoon, Saskatchewan, Canada
Joan Krohn
College of Kinesiology
University of Saskatchewan
Saskatoon, Saskatchewan, Canada

ABSTRACT

Project Move (PM) is a practical learning opportunity for university students in teacher education. Students practice the teaching of dance to elementary school children as part of the physical education curriculum. Each year approximately 65 university students deliver this curriculum based program to over 2,000 school children from Kindergarten to Grade 8. PM participants gain knowledge in curriculum and in the application of effective pedagogical strategies within this unique discipline. In this study of PM, growth in personal teaching confidence was a primary outcome for pre-service teachers as a result of their experiences in the project.

INTRODUCTION

Project Move (PM) is an award winning initiative in curriculum and instruction that began eight years ago after faculty members from the Colleges of Kinesiology and Education at the University of Saskatchewan received requests from generalist teachers in our city whose students had spoken of their desire to learn dance. Students enrolled in the above colleges, who had expressed an interest in extending their knowledge by learning to teach dance, and who had studied dance in their academic classes, were trained to deliver curriculum based dance classes designed by faculty members. In the province of Saskatchewan, dance activities are included in both the physical education and the arts education curricula. PM was designed to develop dance instruction competency for pre-service teachers and to provide a positive learning experience for the school children.

The main purpose of PM is to support the collaborative approach to learning dance content and to provide an opportunity for pre-service teachers to instruct children effectively in a practical environment. Promoting increased conceptual understanding of the content and effective pedagogical practices among PM teachers encourages successful opportunities in the implementation and acceptance of dance in the schools as both an aesthetic and physical form of movement.

History of Project Move

Eight years ago there was a group of boys aged 8-14 from an inner city school who wanted to learn how to rap dance. The principal sought the expertise of physical educators and dance specialists at the university to help meet this need, and an agreement was struck. If the students attended school, behaved, and did their school work, dance instruction would be provided for them. Faculty members (the authors) and university students who had an interest in teaching these children some dance movements, visited the school for six consecutive weeks and choreographed a dance with the boys. Attendance each week at the school varied from four to eight pupils. At the end of the six weeks the boys were invited to present their dance at a school assembly, and later at the university

School of Dance annual presentation. Their performance was outstanding, and proved to be a major highlight in the lives of the four boys who performed.

The second year we assessed the need for PM by recruiting three teams, consisting of two college students on each team, to participate in a pilot study. We visited three elementary schools in the city and taught a series of three lessons to each of grades 2, 5 and 8 in the three schools. During this time curriculum possibilities were analyzed and pupil responses were gauged. This allowed us to select appropriate music and materials based both on the needs and interests of the school children, and on the comfort/expertise level of the PM participants. Scheduling concerns for PM participants were also addressed. In the third year we created a brochure advertising PM, and distributed copies to the schools. Schools who requested PM were put on a "first come-first served" list and PM was off and dancing!

Project Move Objectives and Philosophy

When PM began, we assessed the *need* for the program and outlined our objectives. Discussions with school teachers and principals gave us insight into their needs and provided the impetus necessary to begin the program. Although dance is a part of both the physical education and the arts education curricula in Saskatchewan schools, teachers are often frustrated by their lack of knowledge and expertise in this area. Therefore, we designed PM to meet several needs, they key ones of which were:

1. *To develop dance instruction competency* for pre-service teachers. When our college graduates would become employed we hoped that the PM alumni would have expertise in this area and would feel comfortable teaching dance within their curricula.
2. *To provide in-service opportunities during the lessons* for practicing teachers. Classroom teachers were encouraged to participate, to learn the curriculum content and to extend the learning opportunities for their children after the PM program was completed in the school. We do not see PM as a replacement for (or a single requirement for) the regular program.
3. *To provide school children with a positive learning experience in dance.* We believe that dance provides an alternative physical activity to competitive sports and games and that it allows students the opportunity to explore both kinesthetic and artistic possibilities in movement.

4. To *provide a wider base of movement opportunity for children through dance education.* PM fully subscribes to Canada's national program of Quality Daily Physical Education (QDPE).

Recruitment and Preparation of Project Move Members

In September of each school year, we the coordinators of PM seek college volunteers for the program by distributing posters, placing advertisements, and issuing verbal invitations to identified physical education classes. The criteria for acceptance into the program are that the students: have completed at least one university physical education/dance class, have the desire to teach dance in a school setting, and have enthusiasm and commitment to the PM philosophy. They must be willing to commit to attending three preparatory in-services in order to learn the curriculum, and to teaching six dance classes in a school. They must also have transportation to and from the schools in which they will be working.

During the first term there have been approximately 20 students involved in PM because many students are out of town doing their teaching practicum in the schools at that time. The second term typically draws more: approximately fifty students some of whom have been previous PM members.

At the first meeting of those students wishing to become involved in PM the coordinators explain the program process, introduce the PM teaching assistant, and obtain each member's university class schedule. The teaching assistant is responsible for coordinating the school visitations with each Project Move team member's schedule. This ensures that no student will have to miss university classes in order to be involved in the program. Partners are selected either by each individual's personal choice, by ability or by their schedule availability.

The partners (identified as team 1, team 2 etc.) will team-teach their classes in the school, because we have found that they typically have more confidence if they are able to teach in a team setting as opposed to teaching alone. This pairing also provides stability to the PM program if one member, for some unforeseen reason, is unable to attend. The coordinators also analyze the students' time schedules in order to identify a time when all members are free to attend the in-services. This time usually occurs after 4:00 p.m. when most university classes are finished for the day. The PM teaching assistant telephones the members in order to inform them of the in-service dates, times and location.

Project Move Team Member Timetable

Name _____ Phone _____ Partner _____

Address _____ Postal Code _____

Time	Monday	Tuesday	Wednesday	Thursday	Friday
9:00-10:00	XXXXXXX		XXXXXXX		XXXXXXX
10:00-11:00	XXXXXXX		XXXXXXX		XXXXXXX
11:00-12:00					
1:00-2:00	XXXXXXX		XXXXXXX		XXXXXXX
2:00-3:00		XXXXXXX		XXXXXXX	
3:00-3:30		XXXXXXX		XXXXXXX	

xxx - indicates unavailability to teach in the schools

At the first in-service the PM team members receive a manual and an introductory letter that provides pertinent information regarding the PM format. The manual consists of a PM Teacher Checklist, some warm-up and flexibility routines for all grades, and the lesson plans that they will use in each of the grades they are teaching. The coordinators, who wrote the curriculum and who supervise the PM teams in the school settings, teach the material that the teams will present in the school. This entire process generally requires three one hour in-services.

The teams are encouraged to meet outside of the in-service times to practice and organize their lessons. They are encouraged to divide each lesson into segments and to take turns teaching the segments (i.e., for one week one of the team members will teach the warm-up while the other member assists, and they reverse roles for the next segment of the class). Each team member is given a T-shirt that identifies them as a PM participant and each team is given an audio tape of music that they will use in the delivery of the program. They are encouraged to supplement the music with some of their own musical choices and to use their own initiative and creativity in presenting the classes.

Figure 1 shows one term's cohort of Project Move instructors. Their enthusiasm is evident!

Summary of the Process

1. *Call for PM team members via posters advertising the program. Coordinators and past PM members also visit pre-identified college classes to explain and promote the program.*
2. *At the first meeting introduce coordinators and teaching assistant responsible for administering the program. Collect information regarding each members' name, address, phone number, student number, available transportation, partner, availability to teach and availability to attend in-services.*
3. *At the first inservice, faculty observe the PM participants for possible partnerships. Manuals, T-shirts and audio tapes are distributed and curriculum, teaching strategies and music choices are both reviewed and discussed.*
4. *The teaching assistant coordinates each teacher/grade physical education schedule with the class schedule of each PM team and informs the schools. The completed schedule, with the times the PM teams are scheduled to teach is distributed at the second inservice.*
5. *Learning to teach the curriculum, identifying any potential problems, and addressing questions continues throughout the remainder of the workshops.*

Figure 1. One cohort of Project Move instructors. After receiving workshop training, the instructor pairs immediately apply their skills with pupils in schools.

Recruitment of Project Move Schools

At the beginning of the school year informational brochures are sent to school principals explaining PM. Schools are invited to apply for the program and are selected on a "first come first served" and priority is given to schools that have not previously been visited. An honorarium of $20.00 per class to a maximum of $300.00 per school (i.e., 8 classrooms =8 x $20.00/classroom = $160.00 for 24 classes) is required from each school to cover the cost of materials and administration of the program. To this point, schools have found this fee to be reasonable.

Once the schools are selected, the coordinators meet with the school administration and staff to discuss the role of PM within the school. This meeting serves to prevent confusion and lays the foundation for the subsequent phase, the scheduling of the classes. The schedule must take into account PM members' university class timetable. This scheduling occasionally requires compromise and flexibility on the part of everyone involved in the program. Schools are sometimes asked to rearrange their physical education classes around the schedule we present. This re-arrangement usually runs smoothly and the schools are accommodating.

Teaching in the School

The PM teams teach three, thirty minute lessons to the same group of students at a participating school. The lessons are progressive in nature and the leaders develop a positive rapport with their students by the third visit. After they have taught the three lessons they begin teaching a new class at a different school. In the new school the team members are assigned a new grade in order to provide them with a varied experience and the opportunity to learn the relevance of the material for various grades.

Teachers at the school and the PM team members are encouraged to work together. If a scheduled PM class has to be canceled at the school the teacher must inform the team members and arrange, if possible, a new time. Likewise, if PM team members have to cancel a class they must contact the teacher and arrange a new time. Establishing this direct link between the PM students and their teachers saves coordinators many "third party" problems and gives the professional responsibility to the student-teachers.

A Sample Project Move (Winter) Teaching Schedule

School _____

Contact/Principal _____

Team	Name	Phone #	Grade	Time	Dates	Teacher
A			8	F. 1:30-2:30	March 20, 27, April 3	
B			7	T. 2:20-3:50	March 17, 24, 31	
C			6/7	Th. 2:20-3:50	March 19, 26, April 2	
D			1	T. 11:15-11:45	March 25, April 1, 8	
and so on.............						

Project Move Teacher Checklist

Before entering the school the PM teams are given the following checklist to ensure that the organization of their classes move as efficiently as possible.

A. Prior to Instruction
1. Ensure you have a written lesson plan, and all resources for the lesson.
2. Dress appropriately (Project Move T-shirt and sweats).
3. Arrive at the school fifteen minutes prior to class. Let the main office know you are there.
4. Secure necessary equipment, set it up and ensure it is in working order.
5. Check the gym for any safety hazards (e.g., equipment left out, plates out of the floor)

B. Instruction
1. Greet students and teacher -- be enthusiastic.
2. Assemble students and present the objectives for the lesson. Instruct students as to your expectations with respect to listening, behaviour, and attention signal.
3. Use an introduction or anticipatory set that will create or arouse student interest.
4. Move into instruction and keep the students as active as possible.

5. Limit the amount of teacher talk.
6. Move around the gym and provide appropriate feedback: praise skill or behaviour, and suggest corrective technique if necessary.
7. When teaching the dance (content) remember the sequence: warm-up, orientation to music, introduce individual steps, join with other steps, put dance together, add partners if necessary.
8. At the end of the instruction bring students together and conduct a formal closure. Discuss content covered. Praise desired behaviours and give them a hint of what is to come in the next lesson. Thank students and teacher.

C. After Instruction
1. Return all equipment to the appropriate location.
2. Lock equipment room and gym if necessary.
3. Discuss the lesson with your partner: What went well? What areas need improving?
4. Establish content of next lesson.
5. Establish 2-3 goals for your teaching of the next lesson.

Student Objectives for Involvement in Project Move

From the ongoing research that we conduct on the PM programs, we find that the student teachers have certain expectations and goals about PM. The following are commonly stated objectives for involvement:

1. *Knowledge*	2. *Curriculum*
• to gain knowledge in curriculum	• to learn new dances and curriculum content
• to gain knowledge in how children move	• to be able to develop own curriculum content
• to gain knowledge in movement techniques	• to select developmentally appropriate activities for particular grades
3. *Instructional*	4. *Personal*
• to create positive experiences for children	• to acquire confidence in teaching and working with children in physical

• to develop management skills and instructional strategies • to learn how to develop motivational techniques in this area	education classes • to work towards overcoming the fear of "making mistakes" during instruction • to work cooperatively with partners • to overcome apprehensions regarding perceived negative student attitudes towards dance

Benefits of Student Involvement in Project Move

Our research on PM to date has revealed several findings related to our student teachers. They are summarized below:

1. University students are provided an *opportunity to practice effective instruction in a practical learning environment.* The process of learning to teach and the role that teacher education plays in that process is a topic of considerable interest (Doyle, 1985). By enhancing their conceptual understanding of the content and the effective pedagogical practices the PM teachers experience successful opportunities in the implementation and acceptance of dance as both an aesthetic and physical form of movement.

2. As post-secondary educators, we are able--through our work in the PM initiative--to *gain important information regarding the effectiveness of our educational programs and practices* (Worthen & Sanders, 1991). By developing new instructional ideas and strategies we are able to replace unproductive pedagogical practices and/or maintain quality programs that work effectively. *PM team-members are able to experience a shift from theory to practice* and we, as university educators, are able to *assess member needs* in the development and delivery of meaningful curriculum.

3. Faculty is able to *assess PM teams' growth in the acquisition of confidence in developing management and instructional strategies* in this area of expertise. As well, faculty is able to recognize team-members' *acquisition of dance skills* and their application of these skills to the teaching situation. College students involved in PM demonstrate a growth in the knowledge and the execution of movement techniques. With this growing competence, comes more self-confidence. With this newly

gained confidence they begin to take curriculum risks by developing their own curriculum content.

4. *PM student-teachers practice various teaching methods* including direct teaching reciprocal learning, guided discovery and exploratory learning. Their personal teaching styles begin to emerge as they conduct their lessons. Faculty observes and discusses these lessons with individual students, and they encourage positive teaching competencies. They also discuss alternatives for improvement in areas of weakness.

5. *PM instructors learn to apply a body of knowledge during their lessons,* and to apply strategies to motivate pupils and to provide successful experiences for both the children and themselves as teachers. Learning to observe movement, keeping pupils on task through careful planning and thoughtful motivational procedures, and providing effective feedback to their pupils are ongoing challenges for these novices, but they improve consistently throughout their experiences. Siedentop (1991) suggests that it is crucial that the professional preparation of physical educators include an understanding of the role that motivation, knowledge and feedback play in that preparation; and our experience with PM bears out this assertion.

6. *The new instructors' immersion into the life of the school* is an important outgrowth of their experience in PM. They observe the school children, the activities within the school, the scheduling obstacles, the equipment problems (e.g., ghetto blasters/sound systems that are inadequate for teaching in the gymnasium), the administrative and professional attitudes towards them as neophyte teachers, the overall atmosphere of the school, and the classroom teachers' participation/or lack thereof during the PM sessions.

7. Students work with multiple grades during their experience, which helps them to *identify preferred grade levels they would eventually like to teach.* They also experience the planning process for physically, emotionally and cognitively challenged children. We emphasize inclusion of all children and we encourage our students to plan for and implement strategies for this inclusion. Working with teacher assistants, who often work with these pupils in the school, also becomes a learning experience for PM members.

8. *Teaching dance in physical education takes the teacher into a unique environment where the pupils' number one objective is to have fun* (Kalyn, 1994, Bean & Kinnear, 1989). PM teachers discover the importance of managing students, pacing the lesson, developing and

enforcing rules, and using attention signals. They learn how to increase activity time to a maximum, to decrease managerial and instructional duties, and to provide a stimulating learning environment. Student-teachers find that dance is an enjoyable movement experience for both themselves and their pupils, and that it provides quality exercise and that it contributes to psychomotor learning.

9. *Team-members are able to experience the planning and execution of a lesson* and to experience how much time is needed and used to teach specific concepts. Neophyte teachers are typically concerned with questions of how much content they need per lesson, the time frame for student involvement with the concepts, and the lesson's closure.

10. *New teachers learn to assess the entry level status of the learner.* In their teacher education courses, student teachers study the growth and development of children and the appropriate instructional activities for the grade levels being taught. The PM program provides an opportunity for this theory to emerge as practice. Typical questions that arise are: "What can the children do?" "What if this is too hard or too easy?" "Will they like it, think it's dumb or be excited about the content?" Student-teachers learn to trust the process and the material that they have acquired from the workshops. They typically have little trouble learning the material; however, when they are faced with teaching it to the children, they often experience different degrees of self-doubt and apprehension about their ability to transfer the information to the learners.

It is worth noting here that we have found that our student volunteers enter the program with relatively high confidence levels, and are generally willing to extend themselves, to take risks in a new area of teaching, and to extend their professional expertise for the purpose of developing their own knowledge. Most of our PM volunteers are not dancers, and for many of them their university exposure is their first dance experience.

We have also found that it is very challenging for them to learn about music, rhythm, choreography and instructional techniques, and then to apply this knowledge in actual physical education classes in the schools, especially when many pupils enter the gym thinking they are going to play games. Nevertheless, we sometimes refer to our volunteers as the "cream of the crop." They are highly motivated to learn and we have found that they consistently meet with success because of their sincere efforts to succeed in the program.

11. *PM teachers learn how to work effectively in a team teaching situation.* They quickly discover how lessons can be strengthened through their pooling of individual expertise. They are challenged to be organized and to contribute equally to the teaching experience. In the vast majority of cases, we have found that our teams work effectively with each other, and the student-teachers often comment how much they learn from each other during the lessons.

12. *Team-members learn about classroom and group-management discipline* within this unique teaching environment. Gymnasium management, use of equip-ment, and class control are all practiced. In our PM workshops we address safety issues and we demonstrate strategies to effectively deliver Project Move to the students.

13. *PM teachers experience success.* The student-teachers invariably express pleasure when the children demonstrate interest in the classes and anticipate their return visits. *We have found that many apprehensions and fears among the leaders are quickly put to rest* when the children experience a positive reaction. As invigilators of this program we point out to the PM teachers, however, that this result is not automatic. It emerges through planning carefully, teaching enthusiastically, using relevant curriculum, knowing the material well, and working diligently to create a positive learning experience for all participants.

14. At the end of PM *student-teachers demonstrate and acknowledge growth in their learning.* Many of their professional objectives are achieved and their personal expectations are met or exceeded. The variety of teaching experiences they encounter provides them with confidence in implementing their own instructional ideas in front of large groups and with different grades. They generally become more confident with their own dance movements, with demonstrating dance techniques, and with encouraging creative psychomotor responses from the children. For example, one team-member said after the completion of her first term with PM, "It is exciting to be able to interact with students in a school setting. Now that I have taught some dance techniques, I am starting to become a lot more confident".

Members also learn about perceptions of time and the duration required to teach specific components of the lesson.

Students stress the value of receiving feedback from faculty advisors and classroom teachers. Teachers in training cannot often absorb the multiple realities of the teaching situation, and they tend to remember only the challenging portions of their lessons. Post discussions with experienced teachers reinforces positive factors in the lesson and PM teachers, upon reflection, begins to realize the accomplishments they have made. One PM volunteer commented, "I was very grateful we got to talk to Brenda. Without her there, I would have thought I was an awful teacher." Another member commented, "The teacher came and congratulated us, so I felt very confident."

"I can teach dance!" This is a recurring statement made by the PM teachers as they move towards increased competence in the practical application and reflective processes of teaching dance education. The PM experiences strengthen their beliefs that dance is an important component of the school curriculum. Due to the positive teaching experiences they encounter in the PM program these neophyte teachers are no longer afraid to use the word "dance" in their teaching content. Figure 2 shows PM instructors in action with a primary-level group.

Figure 2. Two Project Move leaders beginning a session with a group of primary children. All PM instructors consistently reported gaining increased teaching confidence and competence from their experience with the project.

Implications of Our PM Experience for Other Programs

What can other educators learn from our experiences with PM that may provide insights as they seek to enhance their own instructional programs? The following process that we suggest to accommodate your specific needs is not complicated.

1. Assess your need. Who needs your program? What are the issues and the challenges of your participants? What do they need from your expertise? What is the entry level status of the participants?
2. Outline your objectives. This will give you clear insight into your own instructional philosophy and the direction you wish to follow.
3. Design your program. Who are your participants? Where is your site/How will you access the site? Do you have any special needs-equipment, facilities? Are finances an issue for your program?
4. Develop a curriculum or program that you wish to implement. What would you like your participants to learn while involved with your program?
5. Provide schedules for participants.
6. Plan in-services to prepare your participants.
7. Implement your program. Start with small numbers to begin with.
8. Assess the program's progress. What are its strengths and weaknesses? Are changes required? If so, make them.
9. What are the implications for engaging in research and writing in your field?

ENJOY YOUR SUCCESS!

REFERENCES

Bean, D., & Kinnear, S. (1989). An obsession with fun? *Runner, 27*(4), 19-20.

Doyle, W. (1985). Learning to teach: An emerging direction in research on preservice education. *Journal of Teacher Education, 36*(1), 31-32.

Kalyn, B. (1994). *An examination of grade ten female perspectives toward physical education.* Saskatoon, Saskatchewan, Canada: University of Saskatchewan, College of Education.

Siedentop, D. (1991). *Developing teaching skills in physical education* (3rd ed.). Mt. View, CA: Mayfield.

Worthen, B.R., & Sanders, J.R. (1991). The changing face of educational evaluation. *Theory into Practice, 30*(1), 13-20.

Send correspondence to:

Joan Krohn
College of Kinesiology
University of Saskatchewan
105 Gymnasium Place
Saskatoon, SK Canada S7N 5C2
FAX: (306) 966-6502
Phone: (306) 966-6477
E-mail: krohnj@duke.usask.ca

Chapter 3

THE INQUIRY METHOD

Karl Baumgardner
College of Education
University of Saskatchewan
Saskatoon, Saskatchewan, Canada

WHAT IS INQUIRY?

The inquiry approach to teaching can be traced back to the experiences of early civilizations. People of ancient cultures explored their environment to find explanations for phenomena that perplexed them. One of the first words in a child's developing vocabulary is the question "Why?". This natural curiosity encapsulates how to apply the fundamentals of the inquiry method.

Inquiring is essentially a normal thinking process through which individuals explore the environment. A person is confronted by a perplexing situation and then responds by reflecting how to solve the problem or to decide upon a course of action. Some educators have defined inquiry as the application of the scientific method. The inquiry approach, however, encompasses a broader scope than this method, because it consists of a number of considerations that accompany cognitive operations. Beyer (1979) states that inquiry

> . . . requires the individual first to define a question or problem about which to inquire and then to guess at tentative answers or alternative solutions -- to hypothesize. The resulting hypotheses must then be tested (evaluated) against

relevant data. Next, one must conclude about the validity of the hypotheses being tested (Beyer, 1979, p. 26).

The inquirer's hypotheses must be revised, accepted or rejected in the light of new evidence. Hence, inquiry is a cyclical process.

Learners at any age level, who acquire the skills associated with this kind of problem solving, will be able to conduct independent investigations in a wide variety of situations. Experience with the inquiry process will also enable learners to utilize an effective personal decision-making approach.

Unlike the instructor in a teacher-directed process, the teacher who employs the inquiry approach becomes a facilitator of learning, who must be creative in assisting students to define the problem. Thus, the teacher becomes a motivator by raising probing questions to assist learners to consider possible hypotheses and gather and test evidence in order to answer these questions. Rather than being the primary source of information the instructor in the inquiry approach guides the learners in finding information for themselves in order to answer their questions. Therefore, inquiry is a learner-centered method of learning.

THE INQUIRY PROCESS

Instructors can create an appropriate classroom environment for inquiry while using other teaching approaches, including those that are more teacher-centered. While developing a positive learning environment in the classroom, a teacher can also model the inquiry process by exploiting "teachable moments" in order to identify a particular problem or an issue that may arise unexpectedly, and to encourage the group to hypothesize about possible solutions and to provide reasons for their position(s).

This "teachable moment" regarding an issue and its resolution could occur in a variety of settings, such as in individual, small group or large group situations. The instructor could pose a casual question such as, "Which movie are you going to see this weekend? Why?" A greater challenge would be to ask group members what their position is on a current political, economic or social issue that may be related to a particular topic in the course. Discussion of a current issue could deal with an international event or a campus or college incident, provided that it will spark interest among the participants. Such inquiry could be introduced with newspaper articles, video clips or topics of interest that members themselves raise.

During this discussion, the instructor would lead the group through a brief inquiry process, while at the same time providing a review of the basic inquiry skills, such as: sharing information, classifying, recognizing frames of reference, distinguishing fact from fiction and analyzing cause and effect relationships.

Once the group has been exposed to the process, the instructor may decide to use the steps of inquiry in a more formal manner. The basic process of inquiry can be outlined in the five following steps.

1. Identify a Problem/Issue

In the first step of the inquiry process participants must clearly understand the problem. According to the instructor's content area, he/she could introduce a puzzling question or a controversial situation to motivate the group members. Teachers could select a controversial reading, a unique quotation, an editorial cartoon, or a current letter to the editor that is related to the course objectives. For instance, in History or Political Science if the concept "democracy" is being developed, the teacher could consider having the students read an article that is critical of the British Royal Family. The group could first explore and define relevant terms like constitutional monarchy, republic and oligarchy; and then proceed to analyze various issues related to peoples' views on them.

To identify a clear issue, the instructor could strive to narrow the topic to enable learners to take a clear position for or against a particular subject. Thus in the case of the Royal Family issue, the problem to be addressed might be stated, "Should Great Britain abolish the monarchy?" Once group participants gain experience with using the inquiry process, problems can be selected that require more complex hypotheses and arguments.

2. Formulate Hypotheses

After members understand the specific issue or problem to be addressed, they must to elicit a tentative answer to resolve it or a hypothesis to test regarding its nature. Instructors should encourage students to raise and to respond to analytical questions for each hypothesis. General questions might include: Does it make sense? What are the implications of the hypothesis? What assumptions are associated with the hypothesis? Are these assumptions reasonable?

For our example cited in step one, the following questions may be used to ensure that learners have done some reflecting prior to hypothesizing: For abolitionists: Is it possible to abolish the monarchy? Why? What would be the effects of becoming a Republic? For monarchists: How would you convince citizens that the costs of the monarchy are reasonable? How could the monarchy's role change to make it more democratic?

These types of questions are intended to draw upon the experiences, background reading, and interests of students to motivate them to investigate the topic further.

3. Hypothesis Testing

At this stage the learners work individually or in pairs or small groups to test the validity of their "educated guess(es)" to solve the problem. This process requires the collecting of evidence and testing it for bias, prejudices and inadequacies, and for distinguishing between fact or fiction. Learners must then select the relevant evidence and arrange it in a logical manner to defend their respective hypothesis. This step may include translating data from charts, graphs and varied statistics to be added to the evidence.

Learners must be exposed to and assisted to utilize a wide range of applicable evidence. They could probe primary sources by developing and administering questionnaires as well as by using direct interviews with key officials. The internet and available print material are other sources of information. Participants must be familiar with the skills to extract the appropriate data from these sources and to document them.

Students may need certain guide questions to gather, test and analyze the evidence. Some of the following questions could be considered:

- Frame of Reference: Who is the writer or speaker? What connection does he/she have to the story (article)? How could the writer/speaker benefit from a particular decision?
- Fact/Fiction: What bias is evident in the article or report? Compare and contrast three reports on one aspect of the issue. What do they agree on? How do they differ? How does the writer/speaker verify claims?
- Cause/Effect: In the previous example, would abolition of the monarchy reduce government expenditures? How would abolition of the monarchy affect tourist business?
- Assumptions: Does retention of the monarchy enhance government stability? Why or why not?
- Explanation: Would abolition enhance democracy? Explain.

In this third phase of the inquiry process, the group-leader may have to facilitate deductive thinking among the participants in order to analyse the body of information via critical thinking. Also, for purposes of time management, the teacher may have to provide some additional information at this juncture to speed up the process. Learners would be encouraged to raise probing questions and then to use the available data to answer them. If questions can not be answered, more research must ensue. When learner skills are lacking in this area, an instructor may have to model the posing of key questions in order to demonstrate appropriate analysis.

Next, the participants would arrange the evidence in a logical manner to defend or refute the hypothesis. This process might involve grouping or classifying information, selecting relevant facts and eliminating biased or unsubstantiated data. From the example regarding the future of the Monarchy, participants must be made aware of the retentionist views of employees of the Royal Family and others who benefit from retaining the Monarchy.

4. Develop Conclusions

The purpose of the whole process of inquiry is to find satisfactory solutions or answer to problems or issues that confront us. The group leader's role is to urge members to suspend judgment and to reach a conclusion gradually based upon careful analysis of the information, as described in the previous stage. In step four, group members are advised to consider such questions as: What have the facts shown? What has been proven? Do the facts support the hypotheses or must the hypotheses be altered?

At this point students could: (a) summarize the evidence related to the problem; (b) reaffirm the hypotheses with a brief summary of the most compelling evidence; (c) modify the hypotheses according to the evidence; (d) reject the hypotheses and recommend another approach to dealing with the problem; or (e) make a generalization about the pertinent data and consider how this may be applicable to new situations.

For participants investigating the Monarchy issue, one conclusion may be to support the retention of the Monarchy because it is such an integral part of British history and tradition. Further, the revenue derived from tourists who are attracted to the royalty can not be ignored. However, group-members may also realize that the retention of the Monarchy does not prevent democratization of the House of Lords and the emergence of a more personable Queen.

5. Debriefing

It is important to review what the members learned about the issue and to reaffirm the significance of each of the four steps in the process. By doing so, both instructor and learners can prepare for any subsequent inquiry topics. For example, some participants may have spent too much time gathering irrelevant data because they did not fully understand the history of the British Monarchy and its present role. Hence, this awareness would help participants in future inquiry projects to understand the problem more clearly.

At the end of this chapter I present four examples of other possible instruments that will be useful when using the inquiry method. Included are a Current Event Report, an Inquiry Lesson Plan outline, an Inquiry Report Worksheet, and a four step outline for promoting dialectic thinking with the inquiry procedure.

WHY USE INQUIRY?

Before deciding to use inquiry it is necessary for instructors to consider the learning objectives of the session (skills, knowledge, values), the learning level and styles of the participants, and the resources available to teacher and learners. The inquiry process is applicable to any content area and it would enable learners to develop decision-making skills that will have lifelong value. Participants who embrace the inquiry process learn how to learn. By developing their skills in inquiry students become more involved in learning, and in turn these experiences can lead to successful individualized or cooperative learning activities.

Hypothesizing and testing hypotheses involves higher levels of thinking and valuing. In many instances the learners are able to recall or reconstruct experiences that they already have, and therefore go beyond the traditional textbooks for information. They can test hypotheses in a science lab, for example, or they can act as social scientists who use media, interviews, and other resources to solve problems or to clarify issues. Moreover, the inquiry process allows learners to work at their own level of ability and interests as they seek to grapple with a problem.

WHEN TO USE INQUIRY

An appropriate time to use inquiry is with a topic that has no obvious right answer or one that leads to informed people taking opposing sides on an issue. It may be related to a current question having local or international interest, but being within the students' interest level. Any topic where students are required to expand their understanding of concepts by a discovery process would be suitable. Also, effective instructors attempt to elicit inquiry for topics in which learners need to assume a role of "investigative reporter" or "detective" in an attempt to solve a problem or address an issue.

HOW TO INTRODUCE INQUIRY

Because the role of the learner in the inquiry approach is that of an active participant, the instructor may be required to demonstrate how to conduct simple inquiries, and then gradually to initiate members into the process. Casual conversations that illustrate the elements of inquiry in the daily decision-making of students can be starting points. Starters like, "Who is the greatest hockey player?" or "Who has been the most influential politician in Canada?" can be explored.

Another starting approach is to have brief discussions or demonstration within the traditional teaching format in order to describe the steps used with inquiry. For example, with a current events topic a teacher may raise these questions, "Is ____ responsible for ____?" "Is ____ guilty of ____?" Similarly, introducing short investigative exercises to be completed from handouts or implementing discovery activities via manipulative equipment and materials would also enable group-members to experience the inquiry process.

A teacher could begin with problems that require a "yes" or "no" hypothesis and gradually move to more complex problems that require several hypotheses. A key point is that the instructor must be a role model, by raising such reflective questions as "What if ____?" or "Why ____?" and then following these questions with such inquiry procedures as a brainstorming session with the group. Within this discussion learners must be encouraged to continue to raise probing questions and to seek evidence from a variety of sources.

WHAT ARE THE PARTICIPANTS' ROLES?

The learner is actively involved in raising questions to understand the problem, in hypothesizing, and in searching for evidence to test the alternatives. Participants who become skilled in the inquiry process may later select their own topic(s) to examine.

The instructor must develop an open atmosphere that encourages members to contribute to discussion and to analyze emerging data. Teachers must ensure that participants have easy access to the appropriate materials or information and that they have the opportunity to develop inquiring skills. They may also have to select the initial problem for investigation by the learners according to the skill level of the group.

The inquiry process differs from direct teaching. In the inquiry method the instructor becomes a facilitator for students as they negotiate through the inquiry steps rather than being solely a lecturer. Learners new to inquiry may need more direction within the process. All students, however, will need encouragement to pose probing questions and to find relevant information to defend or reject a hypothesis.

The instructor promotes productive discussion and is also a ready resource person. The leader must be flexible enough to assume the appropriate role along a continuum from "directed" inquiry to "undirected" (or open) inquiry. Undirected inquiry requires minimal directions from the leader in settings where group members are skilled in the investigative process and when the time allotted is adequate. Where time and/or skills are lacking, the instructor may need to direct group-members through the process and to provide ready access to information for evidence.

WHAT ARE THE LIMITATIONS OF INQUIRY?

Inquiry requires detailed and thorough planning. I have found that more time is required to conduct it *effectively* than is required for other strategies. Hence, less content and material can be covered. Most traditional instructional materials are generally written in an expository format and therefore require the instructor to exert considerable energy to select possible topics that lend themselves to the inquiry method. Moreover, some topics or concepts are unsuitable for inquiry, especially if the objectives are to master and/or to retain a body of facts in a short period of time. For the inquiry approach to succeed, appropriate information must be reasonably accessible, otherwise students could become discouraged or disinterested if they can not find relevant data.

Inquiry is an effective method of teaching but it functions only under certain circumstances. Despite these limitations, I believe that instructors will enhance their professional competence and confidence by adding inquiry to their repertoire of teaching strategies.

IMPLEMENTATION OF THE INQUIRY METHOD

An old proverb suggests that one diagram is worth ten thousand words. The following graphics are intended to facilitate the implemention of the inquiry method into any style of teaching. The best results are attained by incorporating the ideas into a format that is effective for the individual instructor.

To introduce the process of inquiry, an instructor could utilize brief discussions arising from current issues related to subjects in the course. The "Current Event Report", shown in Appendix A, could be used to summarize a newspaper article or video clip. An assignment in which students must select a news item and complete this chart would enable students to internalize the inquiry process.

The "Lesson Plan For The Inquiry Method", shown in Appendix B, is designed to remind the instructor of the key steps of the inquiry method and to ensure that the appropriate planning is completed prior to the class session. The format of the plan will need to be adapted to the instructor's needs.

By writing an inquiry report, the learner demonstrates his/her degree of understanding of the issue being investigated. A useful guide to prepare for the report is "The Inquiry Report: Worksheet", as shown in Appendix C. This chart allows a group-member to record up to four hypotheses and to report the evidence briefly in the spaces provided. If there is only one hypothesis, the vertical lines could be deleted to provide more space. When topics require more depth, learners would have to improvise a larger chart to meet their requirements.

The last chart (see Appendix D) provides a brief outline of how a dialectic thinking process may be used with the inquiry procedure. The "Dialectic Thinking Process" can be used to teach an issue or problem that elicits two opposing views. The major difference between the inquiry report and the dialectic thinking process is the requirement in the former for students to investigate and understand why each side takes a specific position on the issue. This is a good learning experience to enable participants to become informed, active citizens of their community.

REFERENCES

Beyer, B.K. (1979). *Teaching thinking in social studies: Using inquiry in the classroom* (Revised edition). Columbus, OH: Merrill.

APPENDIX A: CURRENT EVENT REPORT

Date: _____ Name: _____

I.   Problem: What is the problem or issue?
     (Write this as a question)

II. Solution: What does the writer or key person quoted think should be done
     to solve the problem?

III. Evidence: Summarize the reasons or proofs given to use such a solution.

IV. Conclusion: Do you think this plan is the best solution? Explain.

APPENDIX B: LESSON PLAN FOR THE INQUIRY METHOD

I. *Identification*:   Class _____   Time _____   Length ____ minutes

Date _____   Teacher _____

Theme _____

II. Define Problem Background (reading, A.V., lecture)

III. Develop Hypotheses

IV. Steps to Gather Evidence Steps to Test Hypotheses

V.   Solution/Conclusion   Debriefing Content/Process

Materials   Evaluation

APPENDIX C: THE INQUIRY REPORT: WORKSHEET

Write an inquiry report of your own. Use this diagram for your outline and attach it to your inquiry report.

Student _____

I.   PROBLEM

II. HYPOTHESES

III. EVIDENCE

IV. CONCLUSIONS

APPENDIX D: DIALECTIC THINKING PROCESS:
THESIS TO ANTITHESIS TO SYNTHESIS

I. *Develop a Thesis*

Provide participants with information (or have them find it) regarding an issue on which members of society may take divergent views. Students discuss the topic and develop a question to capture the essence of the issue. (e.g., "Should the UN 'enforce' peace?")

II. *Brainstorm the Opposing Viewpoints*

Teach participants to develop analytical questions (individually or cooperatively) on both sides of the issue. (e.g., "What are the UN's mandates? What are precedents established by previous cases?")

III. *Establish the Thesis and Antithesis with Supporting Data*

Members write clear statements of the thesis and the antithesis. Then they record the evidence or arguments for each of the opposing views. (e.g., "Thesis: The UN should 'enforce' peace. Antithesis: The UN should not 'enforce' peace.")

IV. *Test Evidence Against Sound Criteria*

The leader assumes the role of facilitator while the participants develop a set of criteria to judge the evidence put forth by each side. As a starter one should consider: "What are the assumptions of the proponents for each position? Are their conclusions based on factual data or on opinion? Do the proponents have a vested interest in a certain position?"

V. *Develop and Defend a Position on the Issue (synthesis)*

Members should clearly outline the reasons why their position is the most tenable. This is also an opportunity for learners to expand their skills in making value judgments.

Chapter 4

PROBLEM SOLVING LEARNING

Jonathan Dimmock
College of Pharmacy
University of Saskatchewan
Saskatoon, Saskatchewan, Canada

ABSTRACT

Problem solving learning is a didactic method that has been used in several Pharmacy classes, whereby students work on problem sets in groups. In this process, a reading assignment is given in advance and students are expected to read this material and answer a pre-class self-examination. During the subsequent class period, students divide into groups and answer a problem set based on the reading assign-ment. Answers to the problems are given in the following class either by the instructor or by students. Evaluations of student learning are made by the instructor not only by "open book" examinations but also by peer assessment (i.e., the students evaluate the contributions of others in their group).

INTRODUCTION

Before outlining the didactic method referred to as "Problem Solving Learning" (PSL), I present some background to the teaching environment in which I work, and the reasons for implementing PSL.

Students enter the undergraduate Pharmacy programme at the University of Saskatchewan after taking one year of classes. Competition to enroll in the Pharmacy programme is keen, insofar as only one student in four or five applicants is accepted. Hence, the students in the four year course leading to a Bachelor of Science in Pharmacy degree tend to be motivated, competitive, responsive and adaptable to new approaches to teaching.

I teach a compulsory Medicinal Chemistry (MC) course to 75-80 students in the penultimate year of the programme, and I also teach an elective course on Drug Design (DD) in the final year. Thus, my teaching is confined to senior under-graduates who are both gifted and committed. I mention these points since, for example, using the PSL approach may not be appropriate for first year university classes.

For a number of years, I used the traditional approach or a "chalk and talk" method, whereby I placed the information on a chalk board to be dutifully copied down by the students. However, I gradually came to a growing, gnawing realization that there were a number of problems with this approach. In the first place, I wondered if the time could not be better spent than merely having the instructor to hone skills of dexterity with chalk and the students to develop notetaking skills. Secondly, little time was available for the students to think about the subject matter that I was presenting, to ask questions about it, or to discuss the material with fellow students or the instructor. A third concern was that my examinations in the MC course consisted of multiple choice questions. Although this method of evaluation presented novel problems for the students to solve, it also inflicted upon them an excessive emphasis on memorization of the material, and permitted them to select only right or wrong answers. That is, they did not have the opportunity to explain why they had reached a certain conclusion, which, even if ultimately incorrect, would at least provide them some credit for partial correct thinking. Thus, I believed I had reached a plateau in my teaching that required some radical changes from didactic methodologies, including my course examinations.

Several years ago, two specific episodes provided me with sufficient motivation to enact some changes to my instructional methods. In the first case, my attention was arrested while reading the introductory comments of *Lectures in Medieval Church History* (Trench, 1877). This book was written in the 19th century by Dr. R.C. Trench, who at that time was the Anglican Archbishop of Dublin. He was a prolific writer and possessed an incredible wealth of knowledge. Yet, in discussing teaching church history to "girls of the upper and middle classes", his approach to the matter was given in the following partial quotation:

How far the wearers of bonnets would bear the strain of competition with those thus assumed to be in exclusive possession of brains . . . on this I give no opinion; but having regard to receptive capacity, to the power of taking in, assimilating, and intelligently reproducing, what is set before them, my conviction is . . . that there is no need to break the bread of knowledge smaller for young women than young men . . . (Trench, 1877, p.vii).

A red flag was raised for me: "Is this all there is to teaching? Namely, to have students receive, assimilate and reproduce knowledge?" I wondered.

The second episode was the visits of an educational consultant, Dr. L. Curry, to the College, in 1994 and 1995 in order to discuss with faculty the incorporation of various changes in teaching methods in a new curriculum.

Curry introduced and emphasized the use of "Problem Based Learning" (PBL). She explained that this approach involved presenting a problem to students before they had learned the basic concept of the topic in question (Culbertson, Kale, & Jarvi, 1997). However, my preference had been the alternative strategy of first providing the information followed by the posing of different questions. Yet, Dr. Curry encouraged me to implement an approach that would provide students with essential information, but would leave as much of the allocated class time as possible for the students in small groups to discuss problems based on the material. Consequently, I began initiating the PSL method based on my initial discussion with Dr. Curry. Later, I also became aware of a similar approach to teaching in a School of Nursing in Wales which was also called PSL; consequently, I formally attached this name to the course in our College.

TEACHING BY PROBLEM SOLVING LEARNING

The procedure I follow in teaching by PSL is presented below.

1. *Division of the class into groups.* The first action to be taken prior to the beginning of the academic year is for the students in the class to be divided into groups. This decision is based on their academic performance in previous chemistry courses. In the case of the MC class, students are placed into groups based on their grades in an Organic Chemistry course that was taken earlier in their studies. Because each group contains a blend of those who obtained above average, satisfactory and below average marks, the groups tend to have a similar range of ability, in order that the weaker students can be assisted by those who are more fluent in the subject matter.

Moreover, the names of students in each group are presented in alphabetical order, which therefore provides no information as to previous achievement levels.

All students remain in the assigned group for the entire course. A similar situation prevails in the DD course except that the division of the class is based on students' performance in the MC course taken the previous year. In my opinion, the ideal size of the groups for both of these classes is 4 students; however, because of our current lack of available small rooms in our building means a typical MC class of 75-80 students is divided into nine groups each containing 8-9 students.

2. *Introductory booklet.* At the commencement of the first lecture in each course, I distribute an introductory booklet, which presents the objectives, the program format and the course outline. As well it identifies some of the relevant resource materials available in the libraries, the key details of the course examinations, and some additional general course information. At this time, I also direct students to purchase the class notes either from the Campus Bookstore or the University Students' Society, which provides the duplicated notes. In addition, I give the first reading assignment that consists of some six pages.

3. *Class notes.* The set of class notes comprises the textual material for the entire course. These typed notes are pre-punched, enabling students to store this material in a binder. The notes are divided in such a way that each of the reading assignments is equivalent in content to the material covered in one 80 minute class-period.

At the end of each reading assignment is a "Pre-class Self Examination" (PCSE). The questions in each of these exams ultimately serves as an indicator to students of how well they have understood the material; and the questions also may provide assistance in preparing students for working on the specific problem set accompanying each session. Each PCSE is designed to be completed on an individual basis, but if time permits, students may discuss it in their groups after the problem set for each session has been completed.

4. *The problem set.* At this point in the process, students will have been given a reading assignment at the beginning of the previous class-period. This reading task, along with the accompanying PCSE, should have been completed. Then, during the subsequent class, each student will receive a designated problem set and will meet in their groups to work on the prescribed assignment.

The nature of the problem set will vary. Generally, the questions are based on the class notes. For example, if the principles of the solubilities of organic compounds was the subject of the reading assignment, students will be presented with the structures of a sample of drugs hitherto unencountered, and will be asked to make predictions of their solubilities in pharmaceutically acceptable solvents, such as aqueous sodium bicarbonate solution. However, on certain occasions prior to the groups' tackling of a current problem set, one student in each group will have been designated to obtain specific information from the library (such as the structure of an organic compound), which was not found in the class notes. This information will be required by the group in order to answer one of the questions on the problem set.

In the case of the MC course, there is often only one correct answer to a question, such as when the problem requires assigning the stereochemistry to a molecule or indicating how the drug will react with a certain class of cellular constituents. However, in many cases some speculation on the part of group-members is necessary when, for example, the prediction of a metabolic route of a molecule is required, thus encouraging a variety of plausible answers to be considered.

On the other hand, in answering the problem sets in the DD course, there is little likelihood of the groups producing identical answers. In these sets there are no specific answers to the problems that have been posed. Thus, the questions, for instance, may pertain to the design of compounds that will gradually release an acid, which has pronounced biological activity. Consequently, questions about this phenomenon could lead to a myriad of answers being given, such as controlling the rate of release by steric, electronic and other physicochemical means. Alternatively, an answer may require designing a molecule to react with a specific receptor site, which could lead to an almost unlimited number of ways to respond. Thus, by having to grapple with problems of this nature, students are being taught to think in a creative and original fashion.

5. *Instructor feedback.* At the time that the students in the DD course give their responses to the questions, I have discovered that instructor feedback is important, whereby students' correct answers are applauded, or where students' original thinking has led to erroneous conclusions, they should be redirected in a gracious and constructive manner. I believe that under no circumstances should their creativity be squelched by unduly harsh words from the instructor.

As instructor, I visit each group to inquire if there are any concerns, to ask and/or answer particular questions, and to redirect those who are on the wrong track. Through this process, I have found that the students generally interact well, and that they teach and learn effectively from each other.

For the MC class, I provide answers to the problem set and the PCSE. For the DD course, I arrange that the groups take turns in providing the group responses; and we organize so that these presentations can be delivered by one or more of the four students in the group.

There are reasons for the different approaches in the two courses. One reason is that a number of students in the MC class struggle initially (and some continually) with the course material. Hence, I have found it valuable to allow as much time as possible to be spent in the group discussions. The students may be able to grasp the material more effectively in this collaborative setting On the other hand, students taking the elective course do so by virtue of individual preference, and generally of higher personal ability for the subject matter. In addition, being in smaller groups in the MC course, permits interaction with the instructor and other students to be more facile.

6. *Evaluation of the performance of the students.* The examinations in both courses are "open book" examinations, whereby students have access to the class notes, previously completed problem-sets, and textbooks of medicinal and organic chemistry. A major objective of PSL is for students to be able to utilize information and to solve problems rather than to regurgitate memorized facts, as is often done in the traditional closed book examination.

I endeavour to make examinations fair for the average student who perhaps finds chemistry difficult. In my experience, I have found little is to be gained by setting tough examinations resulting in class averages of 50% - 55%. On the other hand, I do not wish to leave an impression that the examinations always accurately reflect the potential complexities of medicinal chemistry and drug design. To compensate for this factor, I place a bonus question at the end of the examination, which is worth 4% - 6%, which is designed to be answered correctly by students who have a superior insight into the content of the course.

Normally, in each course two midterms of one hour duration and a final examination of two hours are held in the 13-week term. These three assessments count 90% towards the final grade in the course. The remaining marks come from peer evaluations.

7. *Peer evaluations.* In this process the students evaluate the performance of the members of their group. The criteria that are assessed are: the amount of preparation of each member, the nature of each person's contributions to the discussions, the willingness of each member to participate, and the attendance record of each member. Because this element of group responsibility is often new to many of the students, a "trial run" is conducted after 4 weeks of the course, and the anonymous peer evaluations are returned to each student. In this way, group-members gain an appreciation of how they are progressing and where necessary remedial action may be taken.

The formal peer evaluation that counts 10% towards the final grade is then conducted near the end of the term by following the directions shown in Table 1.

Table 1. Peer Evaluation of Group Discussions

1.   Grades should be allocated for each member of the discussion group except themselves in each of the following four categories listed below. These grades should be out of 10 per category (i.e., a maximum of 40 points is possible).

Category A: Preparation: Has the student read the class notes and understood the material? Was the PCSE completed and if so, how was it undertaken?

Category B: Discussion: Was there a willingness to contribute to the group discussion or not?

Category C: Value of contribution: What was the value of the verbal contribution to the group? Were the comments correct and/or constructive?

Category D: Attendance: In this regard, absenteeism should be noted on the basis of the loss of 1 mark per absence unless reasonable excuses were proffered. It is expected that students will be firm and allocate the appropriate marks since PSL depends significantly on the input of *all* members of each group.

2.   This peer evaluation is part of the student's training for professional responsibilities when, in the future, assessment of others with whom one works will be necessary. This evaluation must be fair, honest and impartial. For those students who have taken their responsibilities seriously and have made sustained, significant efforts to solve the problems, high grades should be given. Conversely, students who have displayed inertia regularly and/or been inconsistent in their attendance should be allocated grades which reflect these shortcomings.

3.   Any evaluation in which all students in the group are awarded full grades will be rejected.

4.   The evaluation should be completed independently and definitely *not* be completed in the groups. After completion and signature, it should be placed under the door of THORV. 216 BY *5 P.M. Friday, December 5, 1997*. Students will lose 3 of the available 10 marks if the peer evaluations are late.

While students may or may not find this responsibility distasteful, knowing how to participate in peer evaluations is part of a key training process. The vast majority of graduate pharmacists in their respective workplaces will eventually be called upon to evaluate their colleagues or undergraduates carrying out their practical training under their guidance. Thus, the use of the peer evaluation process not only enhances motivation in my courses, but it provides prospective graduates with valid experience for their future careers.

BENEFITS OF AND DIFFICULTIES WITH PSL

From my experience using PSL, I perceive at least three benefits from its application to my teaching. First, whenever I have implemented it, the students seem to enjoy the interactions in the small groups: they teach each other and learn together. It has proven to facilitate an active learning process rather than to reproduce the traditionally passive approach of notetaking. Second, I believe that student retention of the material is greater with PSL than occurs with a number of other teaching methods. I show this relationship in Table 2. I also found that in occasional situations when a group may wrestle with and think about a problem for a while and draw an erroneous conclusion that a certain benefit is possible. It is likely that when the correct answer is later given during our debriefing session, the students will take notice of it to a greater degree than if they passively heard the material in a lecture. This is so because of the cognitive, emotional and social effort they had previously expended on attempting to solve it.

Table 2. Teaching Format and Retention

Teaching Format	Retention
Lecture	5%
Reading	10%
Audio-Visual	15%
Demonstration	30%
Discussion Groups	50%
Practice by Doing	75%
Teaching Others	90%

Note. Adapted from Farquaharson (1998).

Third, PSL will prepare pharmacy students for their participation as a member of a health sciences team in whatever career path they choose, in which working together with a view to solving various problems takes place. In other words, the interactions in groups (as well as peer evaluations needed) afford excellent training for professional responsibilities.

What are some of the difficulties noted with PSL? The American humorist, W.C. Fields, in his monograph entitled "Fields for President" entitled the third chapter as "How to beat the federal income tax - and what to see and do at Alcatraz" (Fields, 1971, p. 43).

Beneath the humour lies the reality that while something may be a good idea in theory, practical realities may prove otherwise. Nothing is perfect in this imperfect world. A principle drawback noted in this method of teaching relates to those few students whose commitment to active group participation is either poor or non-existent. For example, in teaching the drug design course to final year students on one occasion, I distributed the questions and told the students that they could either work on their own or in groups of their own choosing. At the conclusion of the course, there were no peer evaluations. Two problems had arisen. In the first place, absenteeism grew, whereby approximately one-third of the class were missing; and secondly, very few of those who did attend the class had completed the exercises. It seemed that the majority of the class were content to wait for the instructor to give the answers to the questions posed.

As a result of this early experience, I implemented a more structured arrangement in DD as I indicated earlier. Being disappointed that students did not handle the freedom in a more mature fashion, I realized that this approach was new to many of them. Thus, I compensated by subsequently providing greater structure and more explicit accountability expectations. Also in some of the groups in the MC class, the instructor became aware of a few "passengers" whose input was minimal, but unfortunately whose slack performance was not reflected in their peer evaluations. A possible solution to this dilemma is to continue to stress that participants are to rate each other fairly, but candidly -- using constructive criticism, as indicated in Table 1. Providing students with model samples of both positive and negative evaluation comments might be helpful in future sessions. In any case, this is one area in which further research may serve to refine the PSL approach in the future.

CONCLUSIONS

I present this overview of PSL along with an aspiration that alternate methods of teaching will be considered by instructors at postsecondary centers of learning. It is my belief that students should be exposed to a mosaic of didactic methods that will enliven the learning process for all participants; and that for those students who may subsequently become instructors, an appreciation of different pedagogical approaches will have been gained.

ACKNOWLEDGMENTS

The author expresses his appreciation to Dr. Lynn Curry of CurryCorp for her advice and encouragement of PSL. In addition, Dr. J.L. Blackburn who was dean of Pharmacy and Nutrition at the University of Saskatchewan at the time of inauguration of PSL by the author gave his enthusiastic support to the project. Mrs. Z. Dziadyk and Mrs. S. Thiessen typed the class notes from material of dubious legibility and are thanked for their expertise and endurance. Finally the author is grateful to his wife Dr. Elizabeth Dimmock who has acted as a sounding board for a number of the ideas on teaching over many years.

REFERENCES

Culbertson, V.L., Kale, M., & Jarvi, E.J. (1997). Problem-based learning: A tutorial model incorporating pharmaceutical diagnosis. *American Journal of Pharmaceutical Education, 61*(1), 18-26.

Farquaharson, A. (1998). *Teaching tips.* Learning and Teaching Centre, University of Victoria, Victoria, British Columbia, Canada.

Fields, W.C. (1971). *Fields for president.* New York: Dell Publishing Company.

Trench, R.C. (1877). *Lectures in medieval church history.* London: MacMillan and Co.

Chapter 5

Synectics: A Metaphorical Way of Extending Creativity

Douglas Smith

Department of Curriculum Studies
College of Education
University of Saskatchewan
Saskatoon, Saskatchewan, Canada

Abstract

In this chapter, the author shows how instructors may encourage students to think metaphorically. He shows how to use a series of metaphors to stimulate student imagination and to enrich their creative thinking. Through examples from art, science, and other disciplines, he shows what synectics is, when to use it, how it was developed, what the instructor's role is, what comprises the phases of the synectics process, and how to involve the reluctant learner in the process. The author also provides demonstration examples to illustrate what synectics looks like in instructional practice, and shows how imagination and creativity can be used to extend and to enrich empathy, problem solving, writing, and invention.

Have you ever examined a common object like a stapler and suddenly seen other possibilities in it? What is it like? What does it remind you of?

For example, do you hear how the stapler sounds like a telegraph key when pivoted and tapped rhythmically on its hinge, or how it looks like a cell phone when opened into a straight line and held against the ear? When folded over, it may suggest a diving board, a grasshopper about to spring, or a catapult propelling poisoned darts.

In these cases we are making the "familiar" stapler "strange". We are enlarging our perception, seeing the metaphoric possibilities in an object, or connecting our familiar association with the object to related things that it may suggest to us. Similarly when we strive to understand something new we often try to discover or invent some ways to make the "strange" thing familiar.

For example, when beer or soft drink bottles were sealed with crimped caps, many thirsty inventors discovered "strange" things that could be used as "familiar" bottle openers. Some people opened a bottle with a belt buckle, the edge of a table, or a pair of pliers. Have you ever opened a bottle with an invented opener? Are there other inventions that you have discovered when necessity demanded your effort?

When we deliberately stretch comparisons or analogies from the familiar to the strange or from the strange to the familiar, we are using Synectics.

WHAT IS SYNECTICS?

Synectics (se-nek'-tiks) is making the strange familiar or making the familiar strange. The word comes from "syn," to bring together, and "ectics," diverse elements.

It can also be thought of as a metaphorical way of thinking and knowing, a way to develop group and individual creativity, and a means of breaking mental set and seeing things in a new light.

It is a metaphoric method of teaching that transforms passive, predictable classrooms to exciting places where student creative development is encouraged. It is a desirable teaching method because it creates active student involvement, it involves peer collaboration, and it enhances thinking skills.

Many examples of Synectics are seen in art, invention, science, and everyday life. Borowski (1978), who was a mathematician, philosopher, linguist, educator, and art critic, suggested that an artist or scientist becomes a creator when he or she finds new unity in the variety of nature. He observed, "Every act of imagination is the discovery of likeness between two things which were thought unlike" (Borowski, 1978, p.109).

An artist in the fruit and vegetable section of a food store creates a portrait using a pear for a nose, figs for eyes, pea pods for eyebrows, and cascades of grapes for hair. The inventor of Velcro plucked a burr from his dog's back and as he examined the simple hook at the end of each burr's spine he had the idea of creating a new form of fastening. The architect who designed the first spiral staircase connected the spiral ribbing of a paper nautilus shell to the ascending curve of steps. Moreover, we understand a doctor's description of a leaky heart valve because we can compare the human heart to a pump and we understand the human system of veins and arteries because we can compare it to the trunk, branches, and twigs of a tree.

In summary, most of our knowledge derives from our ability to connect the known to the unknown, like the child who sees multiplication as a "special kind of adding."

Synectics is a teaching method that uses the natural connections or metaphors of everyday thought to extend our range of possibilities. It is especially useful when an instructor and student want to break free from one way of seeing or doing something. Instructors and students locked into single way of perceiving things can use Synectics collaboratively to transform commonplace ideas, elements, and objects into new forms, uses, and frames for addressing problems.

WHY SHOULD INSTRUCTORS USE SYNECTICS?

Instructors should use it because it jars the student out of mental lethargy and develops the creative potential within; it enhances the self-concept when students realize that they can contribute effectively to the learning process of individuals; it allows mistakes, and encourages experimentation and openness; and it accommodates the cognitive, psychomotor, affective, and behavioral phases of learning.

WHEN DO INSTRUCTORS USE SYNECTICS?

Instructors may use Synectics as an advance organizer or warm-up for art, invention, creative writing, or dramatic characterization; as a problem-solving technique in the classroom, staff room, or board room; as a means of exploring historic, political, social, or spiritual issues; or as a way of developing empathy, insight, new perspectives, or new products (adapted from Mills, 1991).

HOW DID SYNECTICS DEVELOP?

William J. Gordon (1979) developed synectics - *understanding together, that which is apparently different* - in the 1960s as a metaphoric means of developing creativity and imagination in engineers, managers, and students. His method contained several assumptions about the creative process, some of which were:

1. *Creative invention is similar in all fields.* He saw no difference between the discovery of the scientist, artist, businessman, or common person.
2. *The dynamics of the group working on a common problem can speed creativity.* This assumption counters the view that creativity is primarily an individual private act.
3. *The creative process in not mysterious.* He was convinced that it can be described and that people can be trained to increase their creativity.
4. *Metaphoric activity is the means of expanding creativity.* He and his colleagues developed a set of metaphor-creating experiences that aided problem-solving and encouraged creativity.

SYNECTIC METAPHORS

Metaphor is used by Gordon (1979) in the encompassing sense to include, simile, personification and oxymoron. Metaphors or analogies establish a relationship, likeness, or comparison of one object or idea with another. When several forms of metaphors are used together, they also introduce conceptual distance, aid in breaking prior mental set and provide time to reflect.

For instance, during the First World War, British armament makers puzzled over ways of transporting personnel and weapons over roadless terrain. They needed some way of creating a vehicle that could supply its own pathway. When one of the scientists suggested, metaphorically, that they needed a portable road that could be continually replace itself like a belt, they suddenly began seeing the possibilities of tracked vehicles. Thus, the first military tank was invented.

Brainstorming and the three forms of metaphor - direct analogy, personal analogy, and compressed conflict - are used in the Synectics model. After a topic or problem is identified, the instructor accepts all brainstormed ideas from students in a non-judgmental manner. She lists all ideas quickly on the blackboard or overhead and allows students to "piggy-back" on each other's contributions. The students may work as a whole class, in small groups, or as individuals to show what they currently know about the topic. Ideas may be expressed in paragraphs, words, sketches or actions. The instructor records the ideas, and asks for explanations of student choice, until all student descriptions about such conceptions as: "democracy," "animal relationships," "characters in a novel", or aspects of any other topic are listed. The purpose of this phase is to generate a set of words that describe the original topic being examined.

Direct analogy occurs when we compare any one idea with another idea from a different category. In phase two, students would be asked to examine the initial field or list of brainstormed words and to create a direct analogy derived from the words. Ideas generated from the first list of descriptive words may be compared with any other category.

For example, after generating a list of words about "wind power," "clear-cut logging," "romantic love poetry" or any other topic, the instructor could pose such questions as: "What animal is like the Chinook wind?" "What machine is like a newly planted pine?" "How is a love like dawn in a tropical rain forest?"

Another example would be for students to finish a comparison such as: "My feeling for her is like a runaway train because . . .".

The task for students is to compare the original description with something from a new category that is apparently unrelated. In implementing phase two, the instructor would list direct analogies contributed by all students, then the whole group would select one direct analogy for examination in the next phase.

The *personal analogy* phase invites students either to become part of the problem or part of the solution. Using the selected direct analogy from phase two, students would offer adjectives describing how they would feel as the object selected in the new category. They would also explain why they felt a particular way. By doing this, students would have a personal identification with something outside themselves and they would begin to develop empathy for others.

For example, an instructor might ask: "How would you feel as a chain saw during a slash-and-burn forest clearing?" And why would you feel that way?" Or, "How would you feel as a discarded Christmas tree recently thrown on the burning heap?" Or, "How would you feel as a wheelchair carrying a paraplegic student who has to navigate a campus without wheelchair ramps, remote opening doors and cut-down curbs?" The goal of this process is to encourage students to have an emotional experience that extends beyond their existing cognitive understanding. Students describe their feelings and the teacher records on the chalkboard or overhead a new word-set listing their feelings.

The third form of metaphor, *compressed conflicts*, is like a literary oxymoron, paradox or word pair that contains apparent contradictions. The compressed conflict combines tension and special insight. "Peace/fighter," for example, is a powerful word combination that would show the tension of a United Nations negotiator striving for peace in a war-torn country. Conflicting word pairs such as "incomplete/emptiness," "armed/vulnerability," and "cautious/abandonment" are examples that may be selected from *any* of the previous word lists. When writing these pairs the instructor may have to adjust the adjective/noun pattern. Students would then be asked to match word pairs from the set of feeling words generated. All paired word-sets would be recorded for all students to examine. Later, they would select one compressed conflict for the next procedure.

Using these three different metaphors would allow learners to remove themselves from the immediate problem being examined. It would enable them to get a fresh view of what is being explored, and as they would make joint contributions to the lists they would be able to build a shared ownership in the creative process.

WHAT IS THE INSTRUCTOR'S ROLE?

By using Synectics, the instructor is able to: (a) create a cooperative, accepting, freeing, or playful classroom climate by displaying an open and flexible attitude; (b) construct appropriate curricular experiences to encourage learner imagination, curiosity, novelty, and inventiveness; (c) recognize learner originality and reward it; (d) act as a facilitator, process guide, and recorder; (e) accept personal insights presented by students; (f) demand respect from all students for each other's answers; (g) avoid imposing instructor ideas or suggestions on learner insights; and (f) prevent put-downs, pre-judgment, or premature closure.

STEPS IN SYNECTICS

After the topic or problem to be addressed by the group is identified, the instructor applies the steps of the Synectics approach by leading students to: (a) describe an original topic by *brainstorming* words or phrases about it; (b) spawn comparative images from different categories that are *direct analogies* to the words in the brainstorm list; (c) choose one direct analogy then to create a *personal analogy* by becoming the object and describing what it feels like; (d) find word-pairs from the list of feeling words, that yield insight in their *compressed conflict;* (e) choose one of the compressed conflicts then to create a *new direct analogy* by creating examples of things that have the similar compressed conflict in a different category; (f) *reexamine* the original topic using any of the newly generated ideas, and (g) *evaluate* the process to see why or why not sudents responded to each step (adapted from Couch, 1993).

SYNECTICS IS A STRUCTURED USE OF METHAPHORS TO CREATE NEW UNDERSTANDING

The Synectics process is represented in Figure 1 by a multi-spanned bridge that moves from a near-at-hand problem, idea or topic to be explored across several analogies, until from a distance we see the problem in a new light.

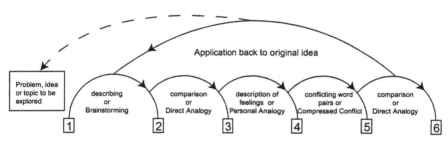

Figure 1. The synectics bridge.

CREATING WITCH CHARACTERIZATIONS: A TOPIC DEVELOPED THROUGH SYNECTICS

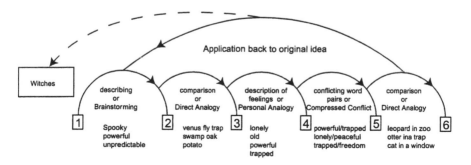

Figure 2. Using synectic structures to explore the charaterization of the witches in *Macbeth*.

In Figure 2, I provide actual examples of word lists generated by students at each of the phases of the Synectics model. The task was to explore the charaterization of the witches in *Macbeth*.

For example, the actor who sees his witch character as "an old sprouting potato" has a rich image to inspire body carriage, movement, speech pattern, and design of costume. Similarly, the final direct analogy of "a trapped otter" suggests new possibilities of flowing movement and a sense of the comic nature of an otter that could be added to the performance of the witch. The metaphoric activity is initiated at each phase after a teacher asks specific questions such as those listed below:

1. What words could you use to describe witches?
2. What plant images do you see as you consider the words in the first list?
3. What do you feel when you become an old swamp oak?
4. What word pairs from any of the lists seem to contradict or be in compressed conflict with each other?
5. What animal could be described as being both trapped and free?
6. How is a witch like an otter entwined in a fish net?
   (adapted from Gunter, Estes, & Schwab, 1990, p.155)

HOW DO INSTRUCTORS INVOLVE
THE RELUCTANT STUDENT?

Because Synectics activities require participants to suspend willingly their disbelief, and to rather use their application of the illogical and emotional approaches, some students may experience difficulty in using the technique. Instructors must be open to this possibility and to explore means of involving the students. A teacher, for example, may invite some timid students to participate by providing verbal and graphic examples of metaphors, or examples of inventions and creative responses from other disciplines. Working with a peer may help other students overcome the feeling that they are unwilling to do something "silly".

Alternatively, to prepare both hesitant and enthusiastic students the instructor may begin with some of the stretching activities listed below:

Making the Familiar Strange

What color is envy? Why?
"Green, because that's the color of jealousy, and everyone is unhappy when they feel it growing in them."
What animal is most like you? Why?
"I am like a male lion because if I roar loud enough someone usually provides for me."
I am like a (name a vegetable or fruit) because . . .
"Banana . . . I'm always with the bunch, tough outside, soft inside."
What machine are you most like? Why?
"I'm like an electric mixer because both the mixer and I like to be in the thick of things and stir things up."

"What-ifs:" Making the Familiar Strange

The instructor could make up a list of class responses to "what-ifs" on the board. Here are a few examples:

What if:
Automobiles suddenly became lighter than air?
We had to live without oxygen?
Buildings could walk?
Vegetables experienced feelings?
Everything turned to salt?
Fish could climb?
Our lawn grass grew larger than people?
We lived in houses designed for apes?
Art were designed to be worn as clothing?
(Adapted from McAuliff & Stoskin, 1987.)

"What-if": Transformations

Instructors could have students: (a) visualize by making drawings, paintings, collages, or three-dimensional constructions; or (b) enact by miming as individuals, pairs, or as small groups of students.

What if:

(Change of scale in Biology) "We were as small as a platelet flowing in a vein?"

(Change of purpose in Mathematics) "An equal sign became a subtraction sign?"

(Metamorphosis in English) "The hero slowly turned into a rhinoceros?"

(Substitution in Art History) "The "Last Supper" was peopled with Rock stars?"

(Changing laws of nature in Physics) "The force of gravity ceased to exist?"

(Multiplication in Sculpture) "People had more than one face, several eyes or three pairs of limbs?"

(Bionics in Genetics) "Humans or animals became part machines?"

(Hybridization in Veterinary Medicine) Horse genes were crossed with those of a butterfly? (adapted from Roukes, 1984)

Space Travel: A Synectics Demonstration Lesson
(Adapted from Smith & Kalyn, 1992.)

The demonstration lesson that follows could be successfully used with students from Art, Chemistry, Dance, Drama, Education, History, Nursing, Education, English, Physics, Physical Education, Veterinary Medicine, and most other subjects. To make the experience relevant, the instructor would need to help students understand how they would be completing an assigned task in their discipline while travelling through space.

After the "Pre-synectics product" and "Breaking mental set activity," the instructor could introduce the topic of space travel in the "brainstorming" phase 1 activity. By referring to global warming and the possibility of earth inhabitants having to migrate to outer space, the instructor could initiate student thinking about a role that they could be forced to take in outer space.

In the demonstration that follows I identify phase titles, instructor directions, practice exercises, examples of student products, and explanations.

Pre-synectics Product

Write a short descriptive paragraph about a space craft or describe a role play, still photograph, art product, or science project that would illustrate a space craft experience. This will be for your eyes only. Just let your thoughts come, then write them down.

Begin now. We'll stop in about ten minutes.

Breaking Mental Set

Try the following for two minutes . . . however, remember this "+" means divide, "x" means subtract, and "-" means multiply. Begin!

4+2=	8-4=	6+3=	12x6=
9-3=	7+1=	7-3=	9x2=
8x2=	8-2=		

Two minutes are up. Pencils down.

I would then explore the notion of "mental set" by posing the following questions: "How did you complete this activity?" "Did you develop a system?" "What was it?" "Did old patterns of mathematical operations interfere with your new task?" "What are the difficulties encountered when we complete a task following directions that are counter to usual practice?"

Phase 1: Brainstorming

List any ideas you have about space travel or outer space. For example, one group of students provided these ideas:

> *"G" force,*
> *blackness*
> *anti-gravity*
> *"weightlessness"*
> *cold*
> *darkness,*
> *astronauts*
> *Colleen McCullough*

Phase 2: Direct Analogies

In this phase we look for similarities by directing the comparison of one thing with another. The group of students in this example decided to compare weightlessness with dancing pop corn kernels.

How is "weightlessness" like a pop corn kernel floated to the surface with carbon dioxide bubbles?

Popcorn, baking soda, and vinegar are combined in a small jar. The acid and base combine to make carbon dioxide, which unites around each kernel. The kernel is then lifted to the surface where the gas escapes into the air and the kernel falls to the bottom of the vessel. The cycle of gas production, kernel lifting, and falling is repeated for each kernel until all the gas is used up.

Phase 3: Personal Analogies

In this phase, students develop empathy and make personal identification with something outside themselves.

The instructor may use his/her voice or recorded music to help guide students through the various levels of personal analogies.

Some students are asked to follow the movement of individual kernels with their hands, others crouch and show the movement pattern with their rising-bodies, still others make the sounds of the lifting kernels, or sound words as the kernels pass to the surface. Other participants who may be accustomed to dramatic action, may join hands to show chemical bonding, then use their joined hands to lift a third person representing the rising kernel. If the group is comfortable with this activity all class members could join in as a type of dance drama. The class could then describe the sensation as kernels moved by floatation and generate a list of words under the personal analogy column.

As an extension in personal analogy, the instructor could have all students be seated. Then using focused imagery, the instructor could use his/her voice to lead the class on a collective personal analogy as space travelers. The instructor's talk might be similar to the following:

You have been selected to be members of the university space mission. This is the blast-off morning. A few minutes ago you bid your last farewells to your loved ones. You have looked at your own home for the last time. Now ,as the elevator takes you up beside the rocket, you experience feelings both of excitement and fear. You know that some space flights have ended tragically. But this is your opportunity, and despite misgivings, you will proceed.

The hatch opens and you step from the elevator into the rocket. You pull yourself up the passage to your seat. You lay back into your seat, you fasten your safety straps. You shut your eyes.

Five, four, three, two . . . You feel a thundering shudder through the space shuttle. Your body is pushed back harder and harder as gravity tries to pull your bones through your back . . . You feel like you can't live if the pressure doesn't stop. It still pulls harder and harder . . . Then finally you have broken free from gravity's grip.

You are in space and as you look back you see the sphere that is the earth gradually separate into colors that show the demarcations of land, sea and clouds.

You gently undo your harness and with the slightest flick of one finger you move off your seat. Your breath against the ceiling is enough to move you toward the floor. You begin to explore your new weightless environment, experiencing freedom from all your normal worries and responsibilities. You carry out one simple experiment that you have designed.

Soon it is time to return to your seat. Again you strap in. The distant round ball of the earth looms closer, closer. It flattens now.

Once more you become aware of the slowing of the shuttle as you re-enter the atmosphere and you gradually descend to the runway.

You take out your log book and quickly record your personal impressions of your space flight. When you are finished you open your eyes and return to the classroom.

Describe your feeling as space travelers or as floating kernels. State the words that occur to you. I will list them on the blackboard.

The students in the example listed:

lonely	*powerful*
stressed	*infinity*
gripped	*freedom*
emptiness	*deadly*
trapped	*closeness*

Phase 4: Compressed Conflicts

Students then selected word pairs from the lists to create the following compressed conflicts:

lonely/togetherness
close/distance
confined/space
trapped/power
restricted/freedom

These word pairs create dramatic tension and capture some of the contradictions of space travel.

Phase 5: Direct Analogy

In the final direct analogy stage the students selected "trapped/power" from the phase 4 list, then directly compared it to a situation with an animal. They used the image of a "chained cheetah" to inspire their final writing.

Phase 6: Return to the Original Topic

Post-synectics Product
In this phase the instructor could repeat the instructions given for the pre-synectics task:

Write a short descriptive paragraph about a space flight or describe a role play, still photograph, art, or science project that would illustrate a space craft experience. This will be for your eyes only. Just let your thoughts come, then put them down. Begin now. We'll stop in about ten minutes.

Students end the session by comparing their pre- and post- writing to see how Synectics had influenced their products.

SYNECTICS AND RECENT EDUCATIONAL TRENDS

Both "multiple intelligences" theory (Gardiner, 1993) and explanations linking "brain research" to "social and emotional learning" (Sylwester, 1995) encourage educators to acknowledge differences in how students learn. Both of these researchers indicate that educational institutions typically emphasize thinking and learning in the areas of language development, logical reasoning, and sequential processing of information. Some individuals, however, prefer learning and absorbing information best through visual, intuitive, or emotional means. Sylwester (1995), for example, warns that when educators separate emotion from logic and reason they neglect a key element in the process. He advocates using activites such as Synectics that provide an emotional context for learning (Slywester, 1995, pp. 72, 75).

Therefore, as instructors, we must consider individual styles of preferred learning, and use different models of teaching that will facilitate these learning preferences.

Creative learning does not mean promoting lack of structure or causing chaos. Rather, creative learning imposes self-discipline. Students are asked to bring their existing knowledge to the learning experience, then to compare personal relationships with the concepts being presented.

Metaphorical learning is accomplished by drawing an analogy between the familiar and the unfamiliar. This comparison helps learners to see both the known and the unknown in a different way. It encourages students to go from the analytical or rational mode of mental processing into the irrational or exploratory mode.

The metaphor is seen as a key to unlock our minds, so that we can go beyond analytical thinking into the world of creative thought and expression. It lets students, themselves, become sources of accepted knowledge.

Synectics is also seen as a bridge, linking one concept to another through a similar connection by using the word "like" to bring new meaning and understanding to the concept. This connection serves to expand and to increase each student's knowledge base.

Thinking in metaphors links the concept being learned with the imagination. The student is encouraged to go beyond what appears to be, or is already known and to ask the question, "What if . . . ?"

By building these bridges we can encourage students to travel into the unknown and explore a concept by means of a meaningful mental journey.

The Synectics process consists of skills that can be learned. Once learned, these skills can provide insight, creativity, active learning and conceptual development - all of which have been shown to yield deeper understanding for the student.

Will you make Synectics a part of your teaching?

REFERENCES

Borowski, J. (1978). *The origins of knowledge and imagination*. New Haven, CT: Yale University Press.

Couch, R. (1993). *Synectics and imagery: Developing creative thinking through images*. Paper presented at the annual conference of the International Visual Literacy Association, Pittsburgh. (ERIC Document Reproduction Service No. ED 363 330)

Gardner, H. (1993). *The multiple intelligences: Theory in practice*. New York: Basic Books.

Gordon, W. J. (1961). *Synectics: The development of the creative capacity*. New York: Harper and Row.

Gordon, W. J., & Poze, T. (1979). *The metaphysical way of learning and knowing*. Cambridge, MA: Porpoise Books.

Gunter, M., Estes, T., & Schwab, J. (1990). *Instruction: A models approach*. Toronto: Allyn and Bacon.

Joyce, B., & Calhoun, E. (1996). *Creating learning experiences: The role of instructional theory and research*. Alexandria, VA: Association for Supervision and Curriculum Development.

Joyce, R., & Weil, M. (1996). *Models of teaching* (5th ed). Boston: Allyn and Bacon.

McAuliff, J., & Stoskin, L. (1987). Synectics: The creative connection. *Gifted Child Today, 10* (4), 18-20.

Mills, S. (1991). *Planning adventures: Synectics.* Regina, Saskatchewan: The Saskatchewan Professional Development Unit and Saskatchewan Instructional Development and Research Unit.

Roukes, N. (1984, March). What-ifs make things happen: Art synectics in action. *The School Arts,81* (7), 18-20.

Roukes, N. (1990, September) Design from nature: From analysis to analogy. *The Journal, 21* (2), 18-24.

Sanders, D. A., & Sanders, J. A. (1984). *Teaching creativity through metaphor: An integrated brain approach.* New York: Longman.

Smith, D., & Kalyn, B. (1992, March 16). *Using synectics successfully.* Paper presented at the Saskatchewan West Winter Institute, Saskatoon, Saskatchewan.

Sylwester, R. (1995). *A celebration of neurons: An educator's guide to the human brain.* Alexandria, VA: Association for Supervision and Curriculum Development.

Chapter 6

COOPERATIVE LEARNING AT THE POST-SECONDARY LEVEL

Sheryl Mills
College of Education
University of Saskatchewan
Saskatoon, Saskatchewan, Canada

ABSTRACT

Cooperative learning is a time honored way to structure classes using the energy of the group to enhance student learning, to increase retention, to strengthen understanding, and to build a cohesive and collaborative classroom environment.

"Make your friends your teachers and mingle the pleasures of conversation with the advantages of instruction."Baltasar Gracian (1647)

*   *   *   *   *

Cooperative learning is an active teaching method that involves students in the learning process directly by having "students work in small groups to maximize each other's learning" (Stark & Lattuca, 1997). Working in small heterogeneous groups, students have two tasks: completing the assignment at hand and maintaining the integrity of the group. There are five main elements in a cooperative learning experience:

- Positive interdependence
- Face-to-face interaction
- Individual accountability
- Social skills
- Group processing

As an instructor of second and third year university students, I have found cooperative learning groups to be a useful way to structure classes. I do not use cooperative learning groups exclusively but rather when there is an advantage or reason for employing this particular structure. Cooperative learning groups provide opportunities for:

- Discussion
- Problem solving
- Consensus building
- Creating enthusiasm
- Team building
- Power sharing
- Mutuality
- Building trust
- Developing collaboration

COOPERATIVE LEARNING AND TYPICAL CLASSROOM GROUPS ARE NOT THE SAME

1. In cooperative learning groups all members of the group share leadership roles; there is no single group leader.
2. A range of ability levels for various skills characterizes group members.
3. Success of one member is related to the success of all other group members.
4. The group is responsible for getting the job done and for maintaining the group; one is not sacrificed for the other.
5. The instructor is a facilitator and does not intervene in the groups unless requested to do so by group members.

6. There is a strong social skills component. Social skills are defined, discussed, observed, and processed.
7. Individual accountability is of critical importance. For instance, students may be required to: sign the completed group assignment in order to indicate their personal understanding of it; take an individual quiz; take a quiz for the entire group; or do a separate, individualized assignment as a follow-up to a project.

Cooperative learning is not a new method of instruction but it has not been as widely used at the college or university level as it has been in the K-12 system. Cooperative learning is neither competitive nor individualistic - two typical features of traditional instruction. In cooperative learning, students are required to interact, to share ideas, and to be responsible for one another's successes. These principles can translate into less direct-teaching time, new ways of grading student work, and increased student ownership of their learning process.

COOPERATIVE LEARNING BECAUSE . . .

"Two are better than one, for if they fall, the one will lift up his fellow; but woe to him that is alone when he falleth, for he hath not another to help him up." (Ecclesiastes 4:10)

*   *   *   *   *

I use cooperative learning groups for a variety of reasons. I find that students better retain information when they have been working cooperatively. Cooperative learning brings a certain freshness to the class. It also brings the students closer together so that our discussions become richer. I often find that students who are uncomfortable sharing ideas in a large group are quite willing to do so in a small group. Cooperative learning "breaks the pace, gives students an opportunity to meet each other, and builds students' confidence in themselves as learners - all requisites of a successful classroom community" (Duffy & Jones, 1995).

Research tells us that students who learn cooperatively "tend to like each other, the teacher, and the subject more. They become more accepting of ethnic, class, gender, and ability differences . . . They engage in more critical thinking and achieve better integration and retention of subject content. They develop higher levels of self-esteem and achieve at a higher level" (Pratt, 1994).

Challenges

There are also some hurdles to cross in using cooperative learning. I have found that students, who have had more than their fair share of individualized and competitive structures throughout their education and extra-curricular experiences, are not always open to sharing their ideas in a traditionally competitive environment. If top grades are a scarce commodity it is difficult to convince students that working together is beneficial. In today's workplace, the ability to cooperate *and* compete is a valuable skill to possess.

Instructors may initially find it difficult to make time for cooperative learning, especially if they have been comfortable with the existing structure of their courses. I have found that the time spent on cooperative learning produces dividends over the duration of the term. Once the students are confident with their ability to work in groups and once they are accustomed to making the make the transition to groups, the time taken to implement cooperative learning groups inevitably decreases.

Another concern among some educators relates to the assigning of student grades in cooperative learning situations. In a pure sense all students would receive the same make for any assignment they complete in a group setting. My experience has shown that this position does present difficulties if the groups are mandated. In my classes I provide students with the choice of working in a group to complete an assignment, with the understanding that the entire group will get the same mark. In an alternate format, one grade can be given for a group project with the students of the group parceling out the marks to each participant as they feel is appropriate.

I have also used cooperative groups for writing exams. I found it interesting to note that the grades for the group exams were more homogeneous that the usual ranges, and that the energy in the classroom seemed higher than was observed for a regular exam setting. Students reported that they learn more from this structure than they did in their regular exam format.

I have successfully used two different formats for group exams. In one format all of the students in the class must agree to this structure. Then they choose their own groups of no more than five students per group, and each group works on the questions in a manner on which they cooperatively decide. Within the time limit, each group finally submits only one paper for grading. All students in each group must sign the exam booklet submitted by their group indicating that they agree with and understand the answers given.

An alternate format for a cooperative-learning exam has both a group portion and an individual portion. Students work in groups of up to five for the first part of the exam, and submit that portion within the given time period. Subsequently, they complete the second part of the exam individually. Students receive this second part of the exam after the first part has been submitted by each group.

In both of these scenarios I permit students who may not choose the group options to work individually, with the understanding that others are working in groups of their choice. Over the years I have observed that certain students have chosen to work independently and I have always respected this decision.

For these group exams, I have found that preplanning is crucial in order for me to arrange the most suitable facility available. Too, I have discovered that it is critical to prepare exam items that lend themselves to a group response, and that it is important for students to be able to self-select their groups. I have learned that this approach cannot easily be implemented on a spur-of-the-moment decision. Careful preparation, organization, and implementation are mandatory.

Cooperative Learning in Action

I have used cooperative learning groups in a number of ways over the years: some simple -- requiring little time to set-up, and some more elaborate. Three types that have proven productive are described below.

Think-pair-share. Students are given a topic or question to consider individually, and then they are asked to discuss their personal response with a partner. Sometimes these "paired ideas" are then shared in the larger group.

Jigsaw. Each student has a piece of unique information for which they are responsible for learning well enough to teach to others. The information packages can either be compiled by the instructor or by the students. Students then meet in groups to teach one another their individually-learned information. This activity can be used for processing large amounts of information in a way other than by lecture. The instructor is thus available to work with individuals or small groups who might need more assistance.

10 - 2. This simple method involves interspersing discussion with lecture - 10 minutes of lecture with 2 minutes of discussion on the topic being addressed. I have found that the short discussion segments helps to lock key concepts into place, and that students experience a break from the rigors of note-taking and listening from afar.

Setting-up for Success

Based on my experience, and that of several of my colleagues, I offer the following seven ideas to aid instructors in structuring cooperative learning experiences.

1. Students must see the relevance of using cooperative groups to learn the material. If there is no reason to use a group then one could not justify its implementation.

Explaining the reasons for using a group makes it more relevant for the class. Students may be required to share limited resources, share information, or complete a part of an assignment.

In one particular class I handed out a sheet of data to each student. They were to respond to some specific questions in groups. People simply processed the information individually; and the groups did not actually function until I took away all but one paper in each group. At that point the members were forced to depend on the person with the "scarce resource" and discussion ensued immediately.

2. Groups seem to function optimally with approximately 2-5 members. In larger groups some students tend to fade quietly into the background allowing others to do the work.

3. Students can find teacher-made groups effective. I typically use methods that randomly group students - drawing names, matching colored cards, using playing cards, matching pieces of a puzzle or incorporating other methods to arrange members that are quick and easy.

On the other hand, in the case of long-term assignments, in which groups are required to work outside of class, I find that students work better when they choose their own partners. Yet, for in-class tasks, the random groups work well.

4. Assistance should be provided if necessary, but enough time should be given for groups to puzzle through on their own before the instructor offers help. For instance, I will assist a group when all group-members request help.

5. Having groups check with each other concerning processes and progress should encourage inter-group cooperation.

6. The instructor needs to circulate and monitor progress as the groups are working.

7. It is important that the instructor provides closure by having groups summarize and share major points in a de-briefing time with the whole group.

Have you ever noticed the effects of a snowstorm on a community - everyone seems to help the stuck car or shovel the sidewalks for others without being asked? The camaraderie that emerges is involved in sharing in a common event or concern. Cooperative learning has the potential to bring out those same feelings -- but hopefully without the natural disaster! Instructors must ensure that the reasons for working together are clear to all participants - that the shared pursuit of positive interdependence is present.

In Summary

Cooperative learning has the potential to bring your classroom to life with minimal changes in structure. By combining rigorous academic elements with the benefits of discussion learning, instructors will promote retention and understanding in an atmosphere of collegiality and cooperation.

REFERENCES

Duffy, D., & Jones, J. (1995). *Teaching within the rhythms of the semester.* San Francisco, CA: Jossey-Bass Publishers.

Millis, B., & Cottell, P.Jr. (1998). *Cooperative learning for higher education faculty.* Phoenix, AZ: Oryz Press.

Pratt, D. (1994). *Curriculum planning: A handbook for professionals.* Orlando, FL: Harcourt Brace College Publishers.

Stark, J., & Lattuca, L. (1997). *Shaping the college curriculum.* Needham Heights, MA: Allyn & Bacon

Chapter 7

THOSE DREADED STUDENT EVALUATIONS: MAKING USE OF THEM

Joan Neysmith-Roy and James McNinch
University of Regina
Regina, Saskatchewan, Canada

ABSTRACT

The study examined the use of the results of mid-term course evaluations[1] to help seminar-leaders improve their instructional skills. The authors demonstrated that this mid-term evaluation can be a valuable tool for improvement of teaching -- provided that leaders act on the findings.

INTRODUCTION: TEACHING AND EVALUATION

In recent years it has been politically expedient for universities to emphasize hiring excellent teachers as well as hiring productive researchers. Emphasis on

---

[1] Evaluation forms, both qualitative and quantitative, as well as copies of the instruments used in this study are available from The Teaching Development Centre, University of Regina, Regina, SK. S4S 0A2. E-mail: tdc@uregina.ca The authors are indebted to Dr. Jeffrey Pfeifer of the Department of Psychology, University of Regina, for his assistance with the statistical analyses in this study, and to Mr. Marc Klippenstein, honours student in Psychology at the University of Regina, for his work in entering the data on the computer.

research has a long history as part of the university "raison d'être" and has been the basis of a considerable amount of support through funding by a variety of research grants from external sources. More recently, however, with the continual increase in student fees, the consumers of education, including the students and the community at large, are demanding excellence in teaching as well as in research.

To demonstrate good teaching most universities have instituted one or more forms of evaluating teaching. As a new faculty member you will likely be faced with an evaluation process for the teaching of each of your classes, particularly within the first semester of your career. As teachers we evaluate our students continuously, but having them evaluate us tends to produce different inner feelings. One of the first questions you will ask yourself is: "What is the purpose of this evaluation and to what use will it be put?" Faced with the evaluation of your own teaching you will no doubt deal emotionally and intellectually with the conundrum: (a) Is this evaluation going to be used to label me as an excellent, a mediocre or a poor teacher for the purposes of tenure and promotion? or, (b) Are the scores and comments provided by the students a useful way of showing me the strengths and weaknesses in this area of my professional life for which I may have had little or no training?

Teaching, like parenting or counseling, is a skill that develops over time. As in any social group, each student within a particular class is an individual and comes to the group with certain skills and expectations. The challenge for the teacher is getting this diverse group to work effectively for the semester in which it is together as a social unit.

KINDS OF EVALUATION

A formal evaluation by students is one way of tracking our progress in specific areas of subject matter presentation and in interaction with students, and monitoring the suitability of the course materials and expectations for individual learners. This tracking may be achieved by having students to complete surveys on our instructional performance. Moreover, the quantitative measures that emerge may show that good teaching takes time to develop. They may also indicate that efforts to improve our style of interaction with students, our presentation skills, and our course organization and management will gradually be reflected in higher quantitative scores on student/course evaluations.

As a new faculty member you might well find that the qualitative open-response questions generally found at the end of many of the standardized evaluation forms are most informative about your day-to-day teaching. While it is true that these "additional comments" usually come from either the very satisfied or the very dissatisfied students, they often reflect strong feelings and reactions to your teaching style.

Typically, course/instructor evaluations are completed at the end-of-semester – a fact which minimizes their rich use as a teaching/learning tool. For example, the instructor will not meet with that particular group of students again, and will not have the opportunity to improve areas needing work for that particular group. Moreover, since no two groups are ever the same, subsequent classes will no doubt require at least slightly different responses.

Furthermore, students typically do not see evaluation of teaching as a tool for improving instruction or for having input into their present situation, but rather as a means of evaluating the person who has had control of the group and material for a semester. Also, students themselves are often cynical about evaluations. Many educators and students frequently claim that such evaluations are meaningless, because they believe that they are not actually read by anyone. Some students have in fact stated that evaluations seem to be given to make them feel they have some input yet, in their eyes, the same faculty members stagnate in the classroom year after year teaching in the same way. Thus, as a student, the best decision is to learn through the "student grapevine" whose class to sign up for and whose to avoid! Unfortunately, all too often these reactions are valid.

Mid-term evaluations are not a novel concept, but neither do they appear to be widely used. Yet they do provide an opportunity first to get to know the needs of a specific group of students in a particular semester and, second, to demonstrate to the students that such an evaluative process can be useful in helping make changes to the course. Using mid-term evaluations also gives you, as the instructor, the chance to educate the students about the complexity of the needs, learning styles and wishes of this diversified group of people we call a "class". Working with the students to find solutions to their diversified needs and interests makes many of them appreciate that there must be "give and take" to try and meet everyone's educational needs.

Research done through the University of Regina's Teaching Development Centre attempted to demonstrate the role that a mid-term evaluation of teaching could play in assisting novice instructors to learn how they have impacted the students, how their instructional skills can be further developed, and how to help students understand the complexities within the content of a particular course.

THE PROJECT

The dynamic and respected instructor of a first year psychology class of 500 students in the institution where the authors work agreed to cooperate in the study. The class met as a large lecture group three hours per week and once a week in small seminar groups of 25 students led by seminar leaders who were current graduate students in the department of psychology. Seminar leaders met weekly with the instructor to review what would be presented in lectures and to prepare workbook assignments for the week's seminar session. Hence, any differences that might have occurred within the individual seminars would have been a reflection of a seminar group's needs and the personality and the preparedness of the particular seminar leader.

Through mid-term and end-of-term course/instructor evaluations we, the researchers, hoped to get an understanding of the effect of using the mid-term evaluation as a tool to help the seminar leader develop skills within his/her own group, and to educate the seminar members in the complexities of managing a group of students. In this way, seminar leaders could learn to make positive changes in the teaching/learning activities during the last half of the course that could lead to better end-of-term evaluations for the seminar leaders and better outcomes in course satisfaction for the seminar members.

PROJECT DESIGN

Thirteen graduate level teaching assistants were hired to facilitate one or two seminar sections of the psychology course. Following mid-term course/ instructor evaluations, seminar leaders were divided into groups. One group of six, the Consulting Group, met individually with the Director of the Teaching Development Centre to review the evaluation results, and to examine possible opportunities for making changes in their student-teacher interactions. A second group of seven seminar leaders, the Control Group, met with an experienced university teacher of psychology to review the evaluation forms and to discuss ways of interpreting these results to the seminar group. No further assistance was offered to the Control Group. All students were given the opportunity to complete the course/instructor evaluation form again at the end of the semester.

A comparison was made between the mid-term evaluations and the end-of-term evaluations to ascertain if the Consulting Group received significantly better end-of- semester evaluations. Since the seminar leaders had a variety of previous training and experience when they accepted the job for the semester, a pre- and post- analysis was made comparing the current end-of-term evaluation outcome of each seminar leader to his or her mid-term record. All seminar leaders were also asked to complete anonymously a short qualitative questionnaire about their experiences of handling the evaluation process as part of their teaching commitment. This form was completed after the final examination results had been submitted and prior to their receipt of the results of the end-of-term course/instructor evaluations.

QUANTITATIVE RESULTS

Analyses of variance were calculated between mid-term and end-of-term evaluations for seminar groups on the overall evaluation and then on the section dealing specifically with course preparation, clarity, and group work, as well as on a section of the survey dealing with qualities of the seminar leaders, such as: openness to students, fairness, and availability. There were no significant differences in any of these areas; however, two positive trends emerged. First, students in the seminar groups whose leaders received specific help learned to appreciate the importance of group discussion more than students in groups whose seminar leaders did not receive the added assistance. Second, those same students rated their seminar leaders more positively with respect to: (a) their ability to present the material, and (b) their availability and openness to their students. A comparison was also made between mid-term and final examination grades for each seminar section, but grades were fairly consistent across all groups and no significant differences were noted.

CONCLUSIONS FROM QUANTITATIVE RESULTS

These results are consistent with those found by other authors who have worked in this area (e.g., Perlman, 1998). In our study, the two month period was too short a time to see more than a baseline measure for change. B. Perlman (personal communication, January 6, 1998) stated that continued work with individual seminar leaders and continual follow-up measures do produce significant change over a longer period of time. He suggests having them work through a minimum of three semesters in order to produce an appreciable change.

The second part of our project analysis addressed the data collected through the qualitative portion of the student/instructor evaluation form and the final questionnaire administered to the seminar leaders. We also examined the directions that these findings indicated for enhancing the teacher-student experience in the classroom.

QUALITATIVE RESULTS

What did we learn from the experiences of graduate student seminar leaders in the program? Basic concerns about their teaching emerged both from the consultations between the seminar leaders and the Teaching Development Centre staff member, and from the leaders' comments provided in the questionnaire at the end of term.

What this qualitative research showed us is that the leaders' reflection both on their seminar experience and on the feed-back they received did help to clarify the dynamics of their performance in leading seminars. These reflections, in turn, may lead the seminar leaders to attempt to become more effective in their teaching. Following are six of the critical issues about their interactions that the seminar leaders identified.

1. *Leading successful discussions requires planning and skill.* This insight came as a surprise to many of the seminar leaders. They found that leading discussions required a considerable amount of preparation - both for the seminar-subject to be discussed and for the strategies required to stimulate and involve students. Many leaders felt that they were weak in this area or were not as effective as they could have been had they spent more time preparing. The literature on this subject confirms that the skills required to present a lecture are less demanding than the skills needed to conduct a successful discussion group. (See for example, Ramsden, 1992 and Brown and Atkins, 1988). Classroom discussion demands a sophisticated grasp of complex interactive and communication strategies.

2. *Establishing rapport with students enhances learning.* Seminar leaders realized that building positive relationships with first year undergraduates was not always easy. They found that the objectives of the seminar, as outlined by the professor, their own intentions, and the needs of the students were sometimes at variance with one another. They learned that careful communication about the design and purpose of the course as a whole, and of its seminar component, improved their rapport with students.

They also realized that first year psychology students in the first semester of their university experience bring with them a certain kind of learning dependence, which made some of the students reject the discomfort of the seminar format and cling to the certainty of lecture notes. Whereas graduate students may often be intrigued by the ambiguity of knowledge and the controversies of conflicting theories, most undergraduates -- particularly when being initiated into a new discipline -- wish to see things clearly and to know with certainty. The leaders found that creating an environment of inquiry and critical discourse in a classroom full of first year undergraduates is much different than "delivering the goods" in an entertaining lecture.

3. *Good teaching requires planning and taking action.* The seminar leaders learned that actually "doing" teaching is not a contemplative or theoretical process; it is an "in your face" activity -- dealing with real people and their concerns, emotions, agendas, and perspectives. This means that group interaction is "complicated activity". A typical first response of frustrated seminar leaders was to "blame the victims", that is the undergraduates themselves, for such problems as: their ignorance and apathy, their lack of preparation, their resistance to broadening their conceptions of psychology, and their stubborn loyalty to the main lecturer (e.g., "But Dr. P. says…").

There were a variety of leader reactions to this perceived negativity. Several of the seminar leaders felt personally or socially (rather than academically) inadequate for the task of leading a group. Several were challenged to try and improve the atmosphere in their classes; others soon adopted a more blasé manner with their students, perhaps as a form of self-preservation. Undergraduates used words like "unprepared", "ill-at-ease", "nervous", "distracted", and "boring" to describe the discomfort that they believed some of the seminar leaders felt or exhibited in the sessions.

4. *The dynamics of successful seminars are complex.* Seminar leaders also noticed that each group is like a living organism, and that no one group will be the same as another. They appreciated that in order for the group to work there had to be some accommodation by the leader for individual differences; however, they were less clear in knowing what strategies to implement to achieve this goal. Some groups greeted the seminar leader with stony silence, which can be un-nerving even for veteran teachers. Several leaders did find, however, that different arrangements of time and space changed the dynamics, and thus they tried to make the classroom space more conducive to discussion.

Seminar leaders also noted how one or two verbal students can influence the atmosphere and rapport of the whole group. They realized that a verbal student, regardless of the quality of his or her expressed opinions or ideas, can be a valuable ally in trying to engage all students in the discussion, but they also had to learn how to place limits on the occasional student who tended to monopolize the proceedings.

5. *Formative feedback encourages reflection on teaching.* Most seminar leaders were aware of the value of the mid-term feedback. They found it encouraging for their morale to hear positive comments from their students, but they found it shocking and disheartening to hear negative comments. However, the latter forced them to look at what they were doing in a new way and did not, for most, allow them to continue without reflectively critiquing the situation.

Seminar leaders reported feeling good about "knowing where they stand". They were able to take constructive feedback provided in consultation with the Teaching Development Centre and apply it in their seminars. One group leader commented that the mid-term feedback helped her with her instructional planning, which in turn helped make the seminars more effective. Another respondent indicated, however, that given the limitations of the course structure, the professor's expectations, and the constraints imposed by time: "I felt I couldn't make many real changes". "Yes", said another, "I had a chance to integrate some new techniques while there was still time to do so".

6. *Reflection can lead to improvements in teaching and learning.* The reflective interchange and encouragement provided by personnel from the Teaching Development Centre during the consulting sessions led the seminar leaders to make recommendations about how procedures might be improved in the future for other seminar leaders in introductory psychology courses. They suggested several modifications, among which were to:

- Introduce seminar leaders to ground rules of class participation early.
- Ensure access of seminar leaders to resources on teaching and on leading seminars.
- Show seminar leaders how to plan flexibly for a complete block of time.
- Spell out to [undergraduate] students what the objectives of the seminar are.
- Encourage seminar leaders to be approachable, relaxed, and helpful.
- Provide seminar leaders with specific skills for working with students.
- Coordinate-ordinate lecture topics with the activities planned for the seminar.
- Organize an initial meeting between the seminar leaders and the Teaching Development Centre staff.

EXPECTATIONS OF SEMINAR LEADERS
UNDERGRADUATE STUDENT

What did we learn from the undergraduates about their views of the seminars? From more than 200 mid-term and 300 end-of-term course evaluations, and the additional written comments from first-year psychology students, we gained some insight into their learning needs and attitudes. Sixty-five percent of those undergraduates completing final evaluations thought that the seminar should be a mandatory part of the course. Many respondents stated that the seminar should be worth more than five-percent of the final grade, in order to increase its status and weight in the overall design of the course. Quite remarkably, in terms of their views of teaching, undergraduate comments were consistent across all sections and could be categorized simply as "expectations" and "appreciation".

Because the undergraduate students had initial learning expectations, they responded negatively on the evaluation forms when those expectations were not fulfilled. To be effective, instructors would need to learn quickly what those expectations are. From the perspective of Instructional Development, the expectations of undergraduates about teaching and learning are not only reasonable, but they constitute basic skills and attributes that all instructional staff should demonstrate in their teaching. Both the negative and positive comments of the students remind us of the importance of intelligent and considerate interaction between student and teacher in an institution of higher education.

The data revealed the following three key expectations among the students.

1. *Undergraduates expect professionalism and commitment.* We found, for example, that they expect seminar leaders to hold regular office hours and to be there when they say they will. Whatever the reason, when someone does not fulfill this kind of expectation, undergraduates tend to assume that there is little commitment to the individual student or to the course or to the learning/teaching process.

On the other hand, graduate students often regard themselves as extremely busy ("overwhelmed" might be a better word), over-worked and under-paid. Their priorities are usually with work on their own research or thesis, but appearing to students to be rushed and too busy sends a strong negative message to the latter. (See also Hendry and Hughes, 1998).

2. *Students expect the seminar leader to be well-organized.* Our data showed that undergraduates use this term in a positive way to describe seminar leaders who gave the impression that they knew what they were doing. This aspect seems to provide the learner with a sense of security; the seminar leader is seen as being

in charge and knows what should be going on. First year students assume that graduate students will lead them into learning with clear goals for each learning task.

3. *Students expect appropriate and timely assessment and feedback.* Unsurprisingly, we confirmed that students expect assignments, papers and exams to be marked and returned to them in a timely fashion. They also expect and need explanations of how to improve their course work. In other words, they expect a rationale for the grading and a consistent evaluation format from one course section to the next, and they want consistency between the parameters for an assignment and the grading of it.

Most of the students' written comments about assessment related to the perceived "unfairness" of the marking system. Usually what this meant was that the instructor or the seminar leaders had not explained the marking system clearly enough. Providing students with examples of appropriate and inappropriate answers to exam questions in advance, as well as extracts from both excellent and poor term papers would all help undergraduates to see the differences between "surface" and "deep" answers. Providing a grading rubric for each assignment would further clarify for students the difference between a failing, an adequate, and an outstanding grade.

UNDERGRADUATE STUDENT APPRECIATION OF SEMINAR LEADERS

The student survey-responses also identified the following three leader characteristics valued by students.

1. *Students appreciate enthusiasm.* In our data negative comments often critiqued seminar leaders for "shyness", or for being "dull" or "boring". Also, several students reported the seminar as being "a waste of time". The converse of these views was a desire to work with a seminar leader who exuded energy, expressed enthusiasm for the subject matter, and demonstrated that he/she liked being in the seminar situation with the students. Such behaviours send a powerful message to students, which is that they are experiencing learning deemed to be worthwhile and validating. First year students appreciate these attributes.

2. *Students appreciate receptivity.* Our findings further suggested that the ability of the seminar leader to be perceived as open and non-judgmental appeared to establish a comfort level in the sessions for all students. The seminar leader who was aloof or blasé had a more difficult time maintaining the conversation equitably in the group. Receptivity is a key to encouraging students to participate

by offering comments and opinions. Students who do so then feel engaged in the learning process in an active way; their learning is validated. They notice when everyone is asked to contribute, and they value the seminar leader ensuring that everyone who desires to participate does so. Receptivity implies a plan to include everyone, as well as an ability to "read the moment". This "with-it-ness" seems to emerge when the leader is prepared and relaxed in the seminar activities.

3. *Students appreciate extra help.* The students who responded to our evaluation survey commented positively on seminar leaders who were willing to help and "go the distance". Students noted acts of leader kindness, conscientiousness, helpfulness, and expression of concern that were over and above the call of duty. Many students in our study saw this caring attitude as the characteristic that distinguishes the excellent teacher from the competent one. Taking extra time to assess a revision of a paper before it is submitted, to provide additional background material for a difficult concept, to let students know they can call the leader at home if they encounter difficulties with an assignment, or to provide extensive feedback on the efforts of a student are all examples of positive behaviours that students identified on their evaluations.

CONCLUSIONS FROM THE RESEARCH

The above summary of the concerns of the graduate student seminar leaders and of the comments of undergraduates in the course confirms what instructors have experienced in their professional practice and what the literature tells us about what students regard as effective instruction. We know that we can improve our instructional performance over time if we ask for feedback about it from our students, and if we heed it.

Alerting seminar leaders in advance to the basic expectations and points of appreciation that students identified in our study should better prepare seminar leaders for the complex task of leading small groups. At the same time, given the complexity of this task and the constraints of time, we must also refrain from placing unduly high expectations on graduate student seminar leaders who, often with minimal teacher training, are learning to teach as they proceed day by day.

This fact in turn raises another question about who would be responsible for the extra work that such good teaching entails. Particularly in a large class with many sections, perhaps there needs to be one seminar leader with a reduced load whose task it would be to coordinate approaches to course assessment and student feedback.

In the process of conducting this research we began to realize that enthusiasm or commitment or lack thereof, were key variables among seminar leaders. Three of the six leaders in the Consulting Group attended only one of the required consultations. Those who came for subsequent consulting sessions tended to be more serious and energetic about their roles as educators.

This inequity of enthusiasm among the leaders skewed the statistical results of the Consulting Group versus the Control Group. As well, there were individuals in the Control Group who were already keen about teaching, and thus sought ways to improve student-teacher interaction on their own. It is also interesting to note that the two seminar leaders in the Consulting Group who showed the least enthusiasm about their role as teacher, were the two whose groups had the largest negative class average differential between the midterm and final examination results.

We believe that if teaching evaluations of a specific instructor are used judiciously they can provide valuable evidence of what goes on in the classroom. However, we think the greatest value of student/instructor evaluations, especially those conducted at mid-term, is in assisting the instructor to understand the teaching/learning dynamics within his/her class early enough to allow for the development of a collaborative atmosphere to achieve class goals.

As a new instructor you might well be asked to teach one of the large first year classes, and then find yourself interacting with and mentoring a group of seminar leaders. We offer the material described in this chapter to help you in this process. By consulting these findings you would be able to help your seminar leaders to understand that your goals, their goals, and the students' goals are all important ingredients to a successful teaching/ learning environment. You could encourage the seminar leaders to conduct a mid-term evaluation and to extract from it useful feedback for their own practice.

Teaching evaluations need not be viewed as a dreaded tool, but rather they can be regarded as one of the few "thermometers" we have to take the temperature of the affective atmosphere in our classes. Conducted at midterm, the survey results can lead to positive interventions for both students and professors. If formal evaluation forms are not available through your particular institution you can refer to several good books on the subject (See for example Centra, 1993). You may want to formulate your own midterm questionnaire to reflect specific issues or interactions you feel are important for your specific class. You might also find the work of Seyer, Smithe and McBeath (1992) helpful in this area.

We have demonstrated in this study that teaching evaluations provide valuable information for instructional personnel, provided that they act on the findings. We have reaffirmed that the reflective use of student feedback can help improve the teaching-learning environment.

REFERENCES

Brown, G., & Atkins, M. (1988). *Effective Teaching in Higher Education.* London: Routledge.

Centra, J. A. (1993). *Reflective Faculty Evaluation.* San Francisco: Jossey-Bass.

Hendry, J.,& Hughes, J. (1998, June). *Roles, Perceptions and Training Needs of Graduate Teaching Assistants.* Paper presented at the meeting of the Society for Teaching Learning in Higher Education, Sackville, NB.

Ramsden, P. (1992). *Learning to Teach in Higher Education.* London: Routledge.

Sayer, P., Smith, C., & McBeath, R. (1992). Developing opinion, interest and attitude questionnaires. In R. McBeath (Ed.), *Instructing and Evaluating in Higher Education* (pp. 319-350). New Jersey: Ed. Tech. Publications.

Chapter 8

TEACHING PHYSICS: VARIATIONS ON THE TRADITIONAL LECTURE

Brian Zulkoskey

Department of Physics and Engineering Physics
University of Saskatchewan

ABSTRACT

Two variations on the traditional lecture, peer teaching and group learning, were used in the delivery of a six-week introductory physics course. The methods were at least as effective as the traditional lecture method of delivery, and the author contends that a refinement of the methods within peer-led discussion, can be more effective than the traditional lecture and can lead to better student performance.

INTRODUCTION

In this article, I describe two methods that I have used in teaching a first-year (freshman) physics course at the University of Saskatchewan. The course is a general survey of physics, and since the majority of the students taking the course are preparing for application to a professional college in the health sciences (Physical Therapy, Dentistry, Medicine, Veterinary Medicine), for most of them it is the only university-level physics course that they will ever take. The stated objectives of the course are:

1) study of the basic principles of physics through a survey of various fields of the subject;
2) study of the applications of physical principles to technology and other scientific fields;
3) development of analytical and mathematical skills; and
4) practical application of the scientific method through laboratory experimentation.

While the first and fourth objectives are of primary importance to a student intending to major in physics, and the second objective is of general importance, it is the third objective that is most important for the students taking this particular course.

The reason that the course is a pre-requisite for application to the aforementioned colleges is that it is hoped that the successful student will have achieved the ability to think logically and to use that logical thinking in problem-solving. The development of analytical thinking and good problem-solving skills in any field requires an understanding of the basic principles underlying that field. This basic understanding cannot generally be obtained by passive means (i.e., by listening and taking notes during a traditional lecture), but rather it requires active effort on the part of the student. Active effort involves reading the textbook, preparing study notes, engaging in discussion of the material, doing practise problems, and so forth. Both of the teaching methods described in this article are designed to encourage (and, in fact, require) active student effort. These methods, when used diligently, should ensure that students are adequately prepared to discuss the current topic when they come to class.

The impetus behind the development of these methods was an article by Dr. Eric Mazur (1996). Dr. Mazur's suggestion is that the students' first exposure to new material should come from reading printed material (e.g., the textbook) rather than from listening to a lecture. Lectures can then be used to give students a sense of what is most important in the material they have read, to relate this to previously studied material, and to check conceptual understanding. Lectures can also be used to paint a broader picture, to relate theories to observations, to provide a different perspective or even to present points that have not been covered in the textbook.

Dr. Mazur goes on to point out that neither teachers nor students expect any preparation using printed material. Students have come to expect what teachers are accustomed to giving, that is a lecture. It will take considerable effort to change this deeply ingrained habit (1996, pp. 13-14). These observations were confirmed by me during my use of the methods described in this article. Dr. Mazur (1997) discusses his own teaching methods in another source, as well.

METHOD 1 - PEER TEACHING

I used this method during one of my Intersession courses, which had an enrolment of sixty. The intersession schedule included two hours of lecture, one hour of tutorial, and three hours of lab or additional tutorial each day for a period of six weeks. Because of the considerable amount of material to be covered in a relatively short period of time, it was essential that the students not fall behind. It was my feeling that they would respond positively to any alternative teaching methods that would aid their performance in the class. Although there was initially some concern expressed by some of the students about the new format (the students submit anonymous weekly comments to me), I proceeded with the method. As mentioned in the introduction, the purpose of the method was to encourage the students to take a more active role in their learning the course material.

At the first meeting of the class the students were divided into groups of four to six. These study groups were then assigned sections of the textbook for which they were responsible to prepare the material for delivery to the rest of the class. In addition to preparing notes from their reading of the textbook, which they distributed to the class, the groups orally presented the material to their peers. Each group then remained at the front of the room and their classmates were encouraged to ask for clarification or to discuss any aspects of the group's presentation. After this, I summarized the material that each group had presented and made additions as necessary to ensure that the material had been adequately covered. I also occasionally did in-class example problems with the whole class based on the material that had been presented, although the groups were encouraged to suggest appropriate examples from the textbook.

Initially student response to the method was mixed. A number of students appreciated the effort to increase student involvement in the teaching/learning process, while others felt that the extra time commitment required of them was not worthwhile. Some students also felt that the student presentations took more time than if I had presented the material, but this latter response appeared to be a problem in perception, because we covered the same amount of material as would have been covered using the traditional lecture method.

Positive student comments about the method included:

> *I like the way you ... involve the class;*
> *I like the peer teaching approach, it offers variety of speaker and causes each student to read and understand the material being covered. To interact in the classroom is far more interesting than just sitting and taking notes;*
> *Class participation is one of the best ways to learn and really understand the material.*

Some of the negative comments included:

> *After a full day of classes, who has time to get together and work with a group? Also, the teachings of the groups are difficult to follow at times;*
> *We have far too much to do already, let alone having to teach the rest of the class;*
> *I feel that the group presentations are a waste of class time.*

As I noted in my reply to their comments, many of the students had not fully understood the peer teaching method. My response was:

> Each student in the class is expected to do the readings of *all* the material, and prepare their own study notes if they wish. Also, in spite of the name of the method, the purpose of the group presentation is to summarize the key points that the group's students had gleaned from their reading of the textbook, *not* to teach the material to the class. Following the presentation, these key points form the basis for a class discussion of the material. Any additional points, plus examples, are then presented by the instructor. Thus the learning of the material involves the whole method, not just the student presentations.

As the session progressed, I noted that the students, who had at first been negative, were more accepting of the method, and it was particularly gratifying to read the following comment in the last set of anonymous student responses:

> *At first I intensely hated the student participation (blackboard presentations) aspect of the course. I wanted to let you know I've liked the classes with student participation after all.*

METHOD 2 - GROUP LEARNING

I used this method during another of my Intersession courses. The class size and schedule were the same as the previous course. This method is similar to the Peer Teaching method discussed earlier, except that the student groups were not required to make class presentations. As with Method 1, the class was divided into small study groups of four to seven students. Each group, on five occasions during the session, was responsible for supplying me with a set of notes that I used, in addition to my own lecture notes, to initiate class discussion on that particular section of the course material. *All* the students were expected to read the appropriate sections of the textbook before each day's lecture. The group of students responsible for a section of one day's material were expected to meet prior to class to discuss their readings and to prepare a concise set of notes based on the outcome of their group discussion. Thus, for at least one section of the course material, the students had the benefit of discussing the material with the members of their group and of possibly gaining an additional level of understanding than would have probably occurred had they only read the material on their own.

The fact that the students were not required to present their notes to the rest of the class is a possible reason why there was no negative feedback regarding this method. One comment that was received (*I'm wondering if you actually read/use our notes during a lecture?*) indicated the importance of ensuring that the students realized that their contribution was significant to the content of the day's discussion.

ANALYSIS

Based on my experience with the two methods discussed in this article, I believe that the first group learning experience, as it evolved during my intersession course, was too similar to the traditional lecture to be effective in encouraging the students to properly prepare for class. As that session progressed, I noted that the students spent less time meeting in their groups. Instead of preparing a set of notes based on their group discussions, most groups sub-divided the material for which they were responsible and assigned a section to each group member to prepare. The result was that each student independently prepared a part of the whole group's notes. Although the students felt that this variation on the method was effective from a time-management perspective, it essentially eliminated the valuable learning that can occur in a small group discussion environment.

Also, because the notes were not based on the outcome of the group's discussions, but rather only on the individual student's reading of a section of the text, the notes were often nothing more than a paraphrasing of the textbook, with important points copied verbatim. Furthermore, I found that class discussion was much more difficult to initiate when the students had to respond to the instructor rather than when they were able to address the members of the group presenting that day's material, as was the case in the peer teaching method.

The peer teaching method had its own set of problems. Because of individuals' variations in blackboard-writing and verbal communication skills, some groups had more difficulty presenting their material to the class than did others. The students were to have read the day's material on their own, thereby reducing the impact of a poor presentation on their ability to comprehend the new material. Yet having to sit through a poor presentation from their peers proved to be a waste of time that could have been more appropriately used by the instructor to give a more efficient presentation.

CONCLUSION

In spite of these difficulties, I contend that some modification of the traditional lecture is necessary to ensure that students come to class prepared to discuss the course material. The instructor can encourage this preparation by resolving *not* to spend time lecturing directly from the textbook. This time should instead be spent discussing, and elaborating on, the key points of the material and doing pertinent examples. To encourage in-class discussion I found that it is essential for the students themselves to lead the discussion, with the instructor acting as moderator. To ensure that the student discussion leaders are adequately prepared, I feel that pre-class small group meetings are needed. Thus, a possible convergence of the two methods discussed in this article would yield a peer-lead discussion, as described in the following section.

THE FUTURE: PEER-LED DISCUSSION

This method requires a modification to the daily schedule described earlier. Rather than having the lecture from 0830 to 1030, followed by a single one-hour tutorial from 1100 to 1200, there would be a pre-lecture meeting from 0830 to

0900, a lecture from 0900 to 1100, followed by a problem tutorial from 1130 to 1200. As was the case in the above courses, the students would be put into small groups and the course material would be divided amongst the groups. Each student would be responsible for reading the appropriate sections of the textbook prior to each class day.

During the pre-lecture time (attendance mandatory), the students would meet in their small groups to discuss the material that they had read. In addition, the groups would be encouraged to prepare a set of notes based on the outcome of their small group discussions. At 0900, the group of the day would give their group notes to the instructor who would then write them on the board or overhead and verbally present them to the class (thus ensuring uniformity of delivery of the course material throughout the session). During this presentation, however, the group would remain at the front of the class, and the rest of the class would then be encouraged to interject with questions to the group as the material was being presented. When discussion of the material was completed, the group would be seated and the instructor would finish the coverage of that section of the course with elaborations, simulations, demonstrations and/or examples, as required.

By encouraging individual reading of the textbook prior to class, allowing time for small group discussions of the course material prior to class, and using class time only for instructor-delivered presentation and student-lead discussion of the key points of the course material it is hoped that this method of peer-lead discussion would make the best possible use of class time and increase the students' comprehension of the course material. I intend to apply this method to my teaching of an upcoming Intersession course. I invite interested colleagues to implement and/or adapt some of these variations in their own teaching practise. I would be interested in hearing of their results.

REFERENCES

Mazur, E. (1996, September). Are science lectures a relic of the past? *Physics World, vol. 9, no. 9*, 13-14

Mazur, E. (1997). *Peer instruction: A user's manual*. Upper Saddle River, New Jersey: Prentice-Hall.

Chapter 9

EFFECTIVE INSTRUCTION: CONCLUDING INSIGHTS

Edwin G. Ralph

College of Education
University of Saskatchewan
Saskatoon, Saskatchewan, Canada

My purpose in this chapter is three-fold: (a) to extract key principles and effective practices characterizing exemplary instruction that the contributing authors have described and/or exemplified in the preceding eight chapters; (b) to identify ways to determine if instructors, in fact, apply these practices in their teaching; and (c) to draw implications from these elements for educators interested either in evaluating and improving their own teaching, or in establishing (or enhancing) instructional development programs or initiatives designed to pursue that goal.

EXEMPLARY TEACHING: KEY PRINCIPLES

A survey of the considerable body of literature related to effective teaching (e.g., Ralph, 1998; Tuijnman, 1996) corroborates both what the authors have described in the previous eight chapters of this volume, and what most instructors have observed in their own educational experience (as students, teachers, and/or administrators). It is almost self-evident among those who have taught any length of time that accomplished teaching is an art, *and* a science, *and* a craft, in which skilled professionals continuously make instructional decisions about both content and pedagogy for the purpose of optimizing student learning.

Proficient teaching is more than correctly performing a set of generic instructional skills -- although these skills are necessary to its success. It is more than knowing one's content, although this knowledge is obviously a mandatory component. It is more than creating a positive and humane psycho-social environment, although such a climate can indeed be "the oil that lubricates" the entire teaching/learning process (e.g., Eisner, 1998; Good & Brophy, 1997).

Both the formal research on teaching and individuals' more informal experiences and observations agree with what the authors of this volume have attempted to demonstrate. This congruency is that exemplary instructors are characterized by several identifiable attributes. I summarize them below (see, for example, National Board, 1994; Wise, 1996).

1. Commitment to Learners

Effective instructors are just as concerned about their students (and their learning success), as they are about themselves and their own instructional performance. Research on beginning teachers' concerns, however, has shown the reverse (e.g., Fuller & Bown, 1975; Ralph, in press): they are primarily concentrating first on "self" (e.g., "Do I appear attractive?" "Will students like me?"), and later, on their professional performance (e.g., "Am I presenting this correctly?" "How is my timing? My pacing? My questioning?").

Then, as novice instructors mature in their professional competence, they become increasingly concerned about students and their learning (e.g., "Are the students getting it?" "Am I presenting the material clearly so they understand it?" "If not, how may I change the factors influencing this understanding?").

A difference between a teacher who functions at a mediocre level of instructional effectiveness, and the one whose work is regularly characterized as exemplary, is typically marked by the latter's consistent and genuine commitment to the educational welfare of the students.

This quality of "concern for the development of one's students" is evident in each of the previous chapters, where the authors demonstrate this caring posture in describing their practice, by virtue of the very fact that they are interested in enhancing students' learning.

2. Knowledge of Material

Accomplished teachers are not only masters of their specific content area, and its past, present, and current concepts, but they possess a general knowledge of contemporary affairs, and of how their particular subject fits into these areas.

They are also knowledgeable about the practice of teaching in two particular aspects. One of these areas is their ability to apply generic instructional skills and approaches that are relevant to the teaching of all subjects (e.g., short- and long-term planning; the structuring/presenting of information; classroom organization and management; oral-questioning, responding, and leading discussions; evaluating student progress; and adapting various methodologies and media to specific teaching/learning contexts).

A second aspect of this teaching-knowledge is "Pedagogical Content Knowledge" (PCK, Shulman, 1987). PCK consists of a set of unique subject-specific instructional techniques or strategies that is particular to certain topics in a field. By virtue of their accumulated experience, skilled teachers have come to acquire this PCK, which is demonstrated, for instance, when an instructor precisely explains to learners how to address a specific problematic area, or when he/she carefully describes how to accomplish a difficult task or to solve a particular problem. Teachers possessing PCK not only know where in a course that students will have misconceptions, but they are adept at providing them with the appropriate degree of guidance to "think through" the difficulty.

Effective teachers' knowledge base also includes an overall recognition of the existing level of the subject-matter background possessed by the students with whom they work, their prior learning experiences, and their specific interests. Although proficient instructors plan, prepare, and present the teaching and learning activities in terms of meeting the needs of whole *groups* or classrooms of learners, they are also cognizant of *individual* differences among students. These teachers are generally aware of their students' preferred learning styles (e.g., auditory, visual, or tactile tendencies); their typical misunderstandings and misconceptions related to certain topics; and their basic motivations toward learning.

At the same time, these instructors realize that it is unrealistic to endeavor to design and implement purely individualized learning programs and/or courses for *each* student within the traditional organizational constraints imposed in the field of higher education. Rather, effective teachers pursue a more reasonable goal: they seek to incorporate a *variety* of motivational and relevant teaching/ learning activities. They do so in order that *all* individuals in the group will (a) eventually encounter one or more of their style preferences throughout the session, and (b) ultimately broaden their own learning competencies by being required to sample a wide range of additional approaches during the course (e.g., Dembo, 1991).

A fourth component of proficient instructors' professional knowledge-base relates to the human aspect of their craft. They make provision in their teaching for individual and cultural diversity, and they treat individuals equitably by avoiding favoritism and discrimination.

They are skilled at creating *and* maintaining a positive and productive learning atmosphere and at establishing a group coherence in which learners' psycho-social affiliation and acceptance needs are met, and where all group-members feel they are worthy contributors to the class.

In the chapters of this book, the authors have demonstrated that they themselves possess the categories of knowledge just described. We have seen that they are: (a) well versed in their particular subject areas; (b) cognizant of the learning characteristics and needs of their particular groups of learners; (c) able to implement meaningful pedagogical approaches; and (d) skilled at creating a positive emotional rapport with their students.

3. Organization and Management of the Environment

A third attribute of effective instructors that has been repeatedly identified in the research literature -- including several of the chapters in this volume -- is their proficiency in maintaining a productive work environment. Expert teachers convey by their professional and personal deportment that: the group has specific goals to achieve; the material to be learned is important; and everyone is expected to perform their share of the work.

These instructors (a) plan activities carefully; (b) prepare necessary equipment, materials, and facilities ahead of time; (c) structure and implement the pacing of the class-sessions to create student motivation; (d) clarify, for the group-members, exactly what is to be accomplished in a particular session, how it is to be done, and how it will be assessed; and (e) monitor the progress and effectiveness of all of these activities, and modify any of them if required.

Skilled teachers also clearly describe the social norms and expectations for the group, and they consistently model these norms, themselves, by means of their own professional conduct. They not only make explicit the basic roles, rules, responsibilities, and routines that will exist in the classroom setting, but they enhance their own professional credibility and authenticity by adhering to these standards themselves. Furthermore, they deal promptly and consistently with the cases that inevitably arise, in which individuals may choose not to comply with these procedures.

When the latter occurs, these exemplary instructors deal with the misdemeanor in an objective and professional manner; and they thus emphasize that the classroom procedures and regulations are to be regarded seriously. Moreover, they have honed their discernment through experience to know when to confront a student who makes an infringement, or when to suspend their judgment rather than to over-react to a situation.

Because accomplished teachers organize and initiate motivational teaching and experiences (for example, by stimulating learners' curiosity, by challenging their existing ideas, by relating to their interests and experiences, or by engaging them in meaningful tasks), they are not often frustrated by the elements that engender group-management problems. Thus, when learners are meaningfully engaged, the following classroom problems are rare: boredom, tedium, irrelevance, unrealistic goals, dull and purposeless repetition, or tasks that mismatch the developmental level of learners.

Again, the descriptions of the authors' teaching procedures and/or their research results in this volume exemplify this third attribute of effective teaching: that of having good classroom organization and management. For example, Gusthart and Harrison found that students desired to have instructors who displayed this attribute; Kalyn and Krohn prepared their Project Move leaders to use such skills; and Zulkoskey, in describing the strengths and weaknesses of his Peer/Group Learning technique, readily identified how to reduce the latter by adjusting the organizational procedures to eliminate future time-wastage.

4. Desire to Improve

Another feature that typically characterizes the work of accomplished instructors is their intrinsic motivation to enhance their own teaching effectiveness. Although they often experience satisfaction for having accomplished a certain degree of success in their instructional role -- whether it is formally recognized or not -- they desire to maintain their effectiveness in the teaching role and/or to improve it.

Because of their ongoing ability to engage in professional reflection and self-evaluation, expert teachers continually monitor the effects of their decisions in the instructional setting: they are aware of their own professional strengths and weaknesses; of what went well or not so well in a particular class session; and of what to do to ameliorate the latter.

As they engage in the often complex orchestration of the many components of the teaching/learning process, they *both* deliberately and sub-consciously model the very skills and behavior that they wish to instill in their students. They do not want to ruin their own credibility by failing to demonstrate consistently the traits and the competencies they envision for the group participants they are leading.

Furthermore, exemplary instructors cultivate their own learning by engaging in such professional activities as: attending and/or presenting at relevant workshops, conferences or seminars; enrolling in formalized graduate programs; reading/studying the professional literature; participating in local initiatives regarding instructional development; or conducting some personal "action research" or "teacher research", in which they investigate a personally chosen question about their own classroom situation.

I can attest to the fact that the authors of the chapters in this book have demonstrated this attribute in their individual careers by not only joining and/or attending meetings of professional organizations in their respective fields, but also by helping to organize, or holding office in, or presenting at conferences related to these subjects.

5. Collaboration with Others

A fifth attribute observable in the professional conduct of proficient instructors is that they cooperate with other professionals in their line of duty. Rare is the image of the expert instructor acting as a "lone ranger," working independently as a solo performer in isolation from his/her peers.

Rather, accomplished instructors typically demonstrate collaboration by engaging in such professional efforts as: conducting joint-research projects, mentoring novice instructors, pursuing scholarly activity with peers, serving on related committees and associations, sharing professional ideas with colleagues, engaging in peer-mentoring activities, or participating in formal and/or informal conversations about the teaching/learning enterprise.

Three examples of this collaborative process are the three studies described in this book that were jointly conducted by pairs of researchers: the "Project Move" initiative by Kalyn and Krohn, the tutorial-improvement study by Neysmith-Roy and McNinch, and the survey by Gusthart and Kelly on undergraduates' preferred traits of good instructors.

Each of these three pairs of instructors worked together to investigate an area of shared interest for the purpose of identifying specific strengths and/or potential improvements in their respective fields of enquiry. They shared their information with us in the foregoing chapters.

Another way that expert instructors demonstrate a cooperative stance is through their collaboration with personnel from the community, who may not necessarily be in the same field. For instance, Kalyn and Krohn illustrated this point in that they worked closely with administrators, teachers, and pupils in several inner-city schools. Indeed, the ongoing success of the Project Move program depends on this key interrelationship with the "off-campus" communities.

Other cooperative ventures regularly employed by effective instructors in post-secondary institutions are: engaging in inter-departmental and/or cross-college initiatives, conducting field trips to relevant sites, inviting guest presenters to interact with their classes, and participating in various academic activities conducted by different ethnic/cultural groups.

EXEMPLARY TEACHING: ASSESSING ITS QUALITY

It is one thing to identify key instructional attributes and skills that are correlated with high levels of learner performance as synthesized above, but it is quite another to identify ways -- upon which all educators are able to agree -- to ascertain these teaching competencies in a reliable and valid manner.

Arguments and counter-arguments ranging along a polarized continuum have been advanced both for and against the setting of teaching standards and their assessment (e.g., Barr & Tagg, 1995; Stewart, 1994). Some educators insist that any attempt to measure and/or assess instructional proficiency will prove to be simplistic, reductionist, behavioristic and restrictive, because they see effective teaching as a complex art and craft that comprises much more than the various implementations of a few generic pedagogical skills (e.g., Palmer, 1997).

Other educators contend that excellent instruction consists of identifiable and observable competencies, skills, and practices (both generic and subject-specific); and that as the research on teaching continues to accumulate, educators are increasingly being better positioned to compare the components of their individual professional practice with the descriptive (not prescriptive) categories and patterns that emerge from the considerable body of research findings on successful teaching/learning (Good & Brophy, 1997; Wiles, 1999)

As with most debates about issues within the social sciences, the best resolution of such issues is one that avoids the dichotomized extremes of the argument, and one that advocates, rather, a more moderate position that may incorporate sensible elements provided by a variety of vantage points (e.g., Gage, 1989).

My synthesis of the recent literature related to the evaluation of teaching in higher education produced the following propositions (e.g., National Board, 1994, Seldin, 1998):

1. Exemplary teaching is identifiable, and the quality of its constituent components can be assessed.
2. A reliable way to conduct this assessment is to collect data from a variety of sources that attest to the quality of faculty instructional performance.
3. Eight widely used sources that have been shown to yield the most valid and reliable results, listed in descending order of use, are:

    *   Student ratings of instructors' effectiveness
    *   Administrator or supervisor evaluations of teaching
    *   Self-assessments by instructors
    *   Peer-assessments by instructors' colleagues
    *   Documents related to instructors' teaching
    *   Informal views from persons with knowledge of instructors' teaching
    *   Other factors (students' grades, enrollments in instructors' courses)

The two chapters in this present volume by Gusthart and Harrison, and Roy-Neysmith and McNinch address how the wise use of student evaluations can provide one valid source of information for decision-making regarding instructional performance.

EXEMPLARY TEACHING: DEVELOPING ITS PRACTICE

To this point I have synthesized the key principles of proficient instruction, and have identified several accepted sources of information used by college administrators to assess this instructional effectiveness. A logical follow-up question -- and the one I pose to conclude this book -- is: What can be done to assist instructors to develop their teaching skills? Or what can educators -- whether they be instructors or instructional developers or administrators -- do to enhance faculty teaching competence? More specifically, what can be done to help the instructional personnel who read this book to implement the approaches presented in it within their own or their colleagues' teaching? I extract three key findings from the bodies of research literature on professional development (e.g.,

Showers, Joyce, & Bennett, 1987; Sparks & Loucks-Horsley, 1999), adult education (e.g., Knowles, 1989; Tuijnman, 1996) and educational change (e.g., Fullan, 1991) in order to address these important questions.

1. *Meeting both individual and organizational goals.* Faculty-members will tend to embrace an initiative if they will reap personal and/or professional benefit(s) from implementing it in their own practice. Moreover, the effort will be that much more enhanced if it simultaneously pursues an institutional goal.

Thus, if individual professors see that improving their own instructional effectiveness will, at the same time, promote the educational quality of the program offered by the department or college where they work, then mutual benefit accrues to both the individual *and* the institution.

2. *Providing consistent support.* A second principle underlying successful professional growth initiatives is that the instructional effort being implemented must be sustained by genuine collaborative support provided both by administrators and colleagues. Instructional developers, supervisors, department heads, deans, and senior college administrators must not only contribute to the professional development program through ongoing "formal" and moral support, but they must also provide tangible, physical and technical support. Allocating the necessary personnel, funding, time, scheduling, materials, equipment, and space/location are also mandatory in order to help sustain the change effort.

"Colleague support" does not mean, however, that all members of an instructional unit will necessarily embrace the initiative, but rather that a core group of committed members will devote themselves to implementing the change and to carrying it through to completion.

Often, when this critical mass of participants attain success in the initiative, then other faculty-members will often be convinced to undertake the change, as well.

3. *Facilitating practice and feedback.* It is true that no one will improve in any skill unless they practice it. However, it is *not* true that "practice (alone) makes perfect." A more accurate rendering of this premise would be: "Practice, accompanied by constructive feedback, makes perfect."

Research on professional development among educators has shown that an effective approach for learning or developing professional skills consists of four phases: (a) a demonstration of the skill presented by an expert practitioner, (b) a rationale for the skill explained by the presenter, (c) an extensive period of practicing the skill by the learner(s), and (d) an ongoing receipt of specific feedback given to the learner by a trusted and credible mentor, coach or supervisor during their practice period (e.g., Showers, Joyce, & Bennett, 1987).

A startling finding that emerged from some of this professional development research is that educators often required 25 repetitions to master the skill during the practice period (Showers, Joyce, & Bennett, 1987, p.86). Thus, in order to internalize the specific instructional competency being practiced -- that is, until the learner attained a point of automaticity with it -- the participants had to be prepared to exert sustained and deliberate effort and to devote substantial time to applying the skill.

But, in the end, is not this effort the critical quality required of *anyone* seeking proficiency in *any* field of endeavor?

It is the genuine desire of all of the authors of the foregoing chapters in this book that interested readers will exhibit this commitment as they decide to incorporate one (or more) of the identified principles and/or practices, en route to enriching their own teaching repertoire.

Indeed, this is the essence of professional growth in teaching!

REFERENCES

Barr, R., & Tagg, J. (1995). From teaching to learning. *Change, 27*(6), 13-25.

Dembo, M. (1991). *Applying educational psychology in the classroom* (4th ed.). New York: Longman.

Eisner, E. (1998). *The enlightened eye*. Columbus, OH: Merrill.

Fullan, M. (1991). *The new meaning of educational change* (2nd ed.). New York: Teachers College Press.

Fuller, F., & Bown, O. (1975). Becoming a teacher. In K. Ryan (Ed.), *Teacher education: The 74th yearbook for the National Society of the Study of Education* (Part II, pp. 25-52). Chicago: University of Chicago Press.

Gage, N. (1989). The paradigm wars and their aftermath. *Educational Research, 18*(7), 4-10.

Good, T., & Brophy, J. (1997). *Looking in classrooms* (7th ed.). New York: Longman.

Knowles, M. (1989). *The making of an adult educator*. San Francisco, CA: Jossey-Bass.

National Board for Professional Teaching Standards. (1994). *What teachers should know and be able to do*. Washington, DC: Author.

Palmer, P. (1997). The heart of a teacher: Identity and integrity in teaching. *Change, 29*(6), 14-21.

Ralph, E. (1998). *Motivating teaching in higher education: A manual for faculty development*. Stillwater, OK: New Forums Press.

Ralph, E. (in press). Helping reduce teacher-interns' anxieties during the extended-practicum. *Teaching Education.*

Seldin, P. (1998). How colleges evaluate teaching: What's new (and not) since 1988. *American Association for Higher Education Bulletin, 50*(7), 3-7.

Showers, B., Joyce, B., & Bennett, B. (1987). Synthesis of research on staff development: A framework for future study and a state-of-the-art analysis. *Educational Leadership, 45*(3), 77-87.

Sparks, D., & Loucks-Horsley, S. (1999). Five models of staff development for teachers. In A.C. Ornstein & L.S. Behar-Horensteinn (Eds.), *Contemporary issues in curriculum* (2nd ed., pp. 295-319). Boston: Allyn and Bacon).

Stewart, D. (1994). Teaching undiminished. *Canadian Journal of Education, 19*(3), 299-304.

Tuijnman, A. (Ed.). (1996). *International encyclopedia of adult education and training* (2nd ed.). New York: Elsevier Science.

Wiles, J. (1999). *Curriculum essentials: A resource for educators.* Boston: Allyn and Bacon.

Wise, A. (Ed.). (1996). Qualitity teaching for the 21st century [Special issue]. *Phi Delta Kappan, 78*(3).

CONTRIBUTORS

KARL BAUMGARDNER - Karl Baumgardner teaches methods courses and is a supervisor of extended-practicum with the Department of Curriculum Studies in the College of Education at the University of Saskatchewan. Recognized by both faculty and students for his professional skills and his supportive leadership, he draws from his own extensive educational background to offer valuable insights in applying the Inquiry approach to enhance the teaching/ learning process. He was a nominee for "Supervisor of the Year" by the Education Students Society.

JONATHAN DIMMOCK - Jonathan Dimmock obtained his honours Bachelor's degree and a Ph.D. from the University of London. After four years in industry, he took up an academic position in the University of Saskatchewan in 1967 where he has taught medicinal chemistry and drug design principally. In 1976 he was promoted to full professor. He is the co-author of a book entitled "An introduction to drug design". In 1998, he was honoured with a Teaching Excellence Award from the University of Saskatchewan Students Union. In addition, Dr. Dimmock has published over 100 refereed papers and has obtained several patents in medicinal chemistry.

LEN GUSTHART - Dr. Gusthart has over thirty years teaching experience at the university level. He became a full professor at the University of Saskatchewan in 1986. He has been recognized as an outstanding university teacher and received the Master Teacher Award in 1997. Prior to joining the university faculty, he was a teacher and school administrator for ten years. He has written or co-written more than 40 papers for journals, published chapters in five books, written a number of technical reports, and given scores of presentations at venues across North America.

PAUL HARRISON - Paul Harrison is a professor in the College of Business Administration at the University of South Carolina. He teaches managerial accounting in the Master's programs in the Darla Moore School of Business. Dr. Harrison's primary research interests are in student evaluation of teaching effectiveness, and escalation of commitment to poorly performing projects.

BRENDA KALYN - Brenda Kalyn currently specializes in physical education pedagogy and school physical education programs and is also a former consultant in the area of movement education and dance. Her interests in research involve teacher education, students' perceptions of their physical education experiences, subject integration and dance pedagogy. She was a nominee for the "Educator of the Year Award" in the College of Education and with Joan Krohn she received the Saskatchewan Physical Education Association Initiative Award for excellence in programming for Project Move.

JOAN KROHN - Joan Krohn specializes in school physical education, pedagogy, and dance education. She has served as Chairperson of Dance Saskatchewan Inc., and is a founding member of Project Move, and P.A.A.L., a program for children with special needs. Her research interests include teacher education in physical education, children's perceptions of their dance experiences, and dance pedagogy.

JAMES MCNINCH - James McNinch is the Director of the Teaching Development Centre at the University of Regina. He is also an instructor of Introductory English and Composition and of Professional Studies in Education. His recent research has investigated issues of teacher identity, and of the learning needs of first year university students. Dr. McNinch started his career as a high school English teacher, and worked as an administrator and teacher in Aboriginal Teacher Education before joining the University of Regina.

SHERYL MILLS - Sheryl Mills, B.Ed, M.Ed, has taught for the past twenty years at all levels of the education system, most recently at the university level. Her classes are active, upbeat and rigorous, and she frequently incorporates cooperative learning in its various forms.

EDWIN RALPH - Edwin Ralph's extensive and varied career in education spans 40 years. A prolific writer, a distinguished researcher, and an award-winning teacher himself, he has a keen interest in instructional improvement (and its supervision) at all levels of teaching -- from early childhood education through to graduate school, including adult education, staff development, pre- and inservice training and beyond.

JOAN NEYSMITH-ROY - Joan Neysmith-Roy is an Associate Professor and Head of the Department of Psychology at the University of Regina. She is also the Chair of the Advisory Committee for the Teaching Development Centre. Her research interests include improvement in teaching in Higher Education, pre-linguistic development in autistic children, and preventative mental health issues in families with infants. Dr. Roy started her career as a high school teacher, and was a school psychologist prior to accepting a university appointment.

DOUGLAS SMITH - Douglas Smith was Academic Coordinator of School Based Programs at the University of Saskatchewan, and currently works in preservice and graduate teacher education. His research interests are in teacher education, teacher supervision, models of instruction, cross-cultural education, and instructional development in higher education

BRIAN ZULKOSKEY - Brian Zulkoskey holds two degrees from the University of Saskatchewan, B.Sc. (Hon.) and M.Sc. in Physics. He has been a lab instructor in the Department of Physics and Engineering Physics at the University of Saskatchewan since 1981, and since 1990 has also been a sessional lecturer for Physics 111. In 1998, following two previous nominations, he was awarded a USSU (University of Saskatchewan Students' Union) Teaching Excellence Award.

PHOTO CREDITS

Photographs of Karl Baumgardner, Brenda Kalyn, Joan Krohn, Sheryl Mills, Edwin Ralph, and Douglas Smith by Jay Wilson, College of Education, University of Saskatchewan, Saskatoon, Canada.

INDEX

INDEX